BEASTLY EDINBURGH

Barclay Price

AMBERLEY

I'm not an animal lover if that means you think things are nice
if you can pat them, but I am intoxicated by animals.

Sir David Attenborough

First published 2022

Amberley Publishing
The Hill, Stroud
Gloucestershire, GL5 4EP

www.amberley-books.com

ISBN 978 1 3981 0730 4 (print)
ISBN 978 1 3981 0731 1 (ebook)

British Library Cataloguing in Publication Data.
A catalogue record for this book is available from the British Library.

Typesetting by SJmagic DESIGN SERVICES, India.
Printed in Great Britain.

Contents

Introduction

In Edinburgh, working animals were once a common sight. Horses kept the city moving and the mooing of cows was a commonplace urban sound. The relationships between residents and the animals that have shared the city have been diverse and notable. An Edinburgh pig carried a duchess on its back; an elephant upset a baker; a cat charmed a royal personage; a dog rejected a bad penny; and a penguin was knighted by a king. This book provides a flavour of Edinburgh's interactions between humans and animals – some involving ill-treatment and others high regard. And as Edinburgh uniquely has five statues to named dogs, one chapter highlights a number of the varied animal portrayals that ornament the city's public spaces.

1. Horse Power

On 26 January 1985, the last horse-drawn milk cart rattled through the streets of Edinburgh, symbolically marking the end of horse-drawn transport in the city. For hundreds of years horses were the most important animals in the city as they moved goods and people in and out of the city, and the sight, sound and smell of horses were an integral part of city life. There were four broad roles for horses: saddle horses, ridden by an individual and by the cavalry; carriage and coach horses; cart and pack horses; and farm horses, mainly used in ploughing.

The layout of the medieval old town, with its single long street and narrow closes, kept horse use to a minimum until the building of the New Town and the wider city expansion. The 1788 record for horse tax payments, a tax introduced a few years earlier to help pay for the war against France, lists 347 horses owned in the city with its then population of 57,000. Many of these horses were kept in the stables that were part of the grander houses in the old town. Horses that were stabled on their own or not regularly taken out for exercise often became fractious. Some developed bad habits such as kicking the walls of the stall with the hind feet or biting on the feeding box. Horses that were content in their stable often came to know the way home and it was not unknown for a rider to doze off, leaving the horse to navigate the way back. Other horses were kept in the fields that surrounded the

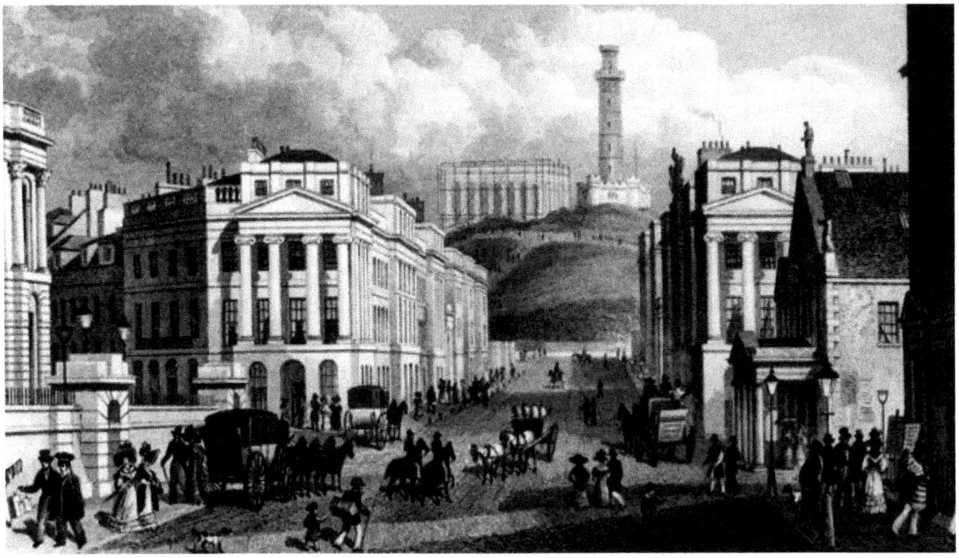

Waterloo Place looking to Calton Hill by T. Barber (from a painting by Thomas Hosmer Shepherd, 1829).

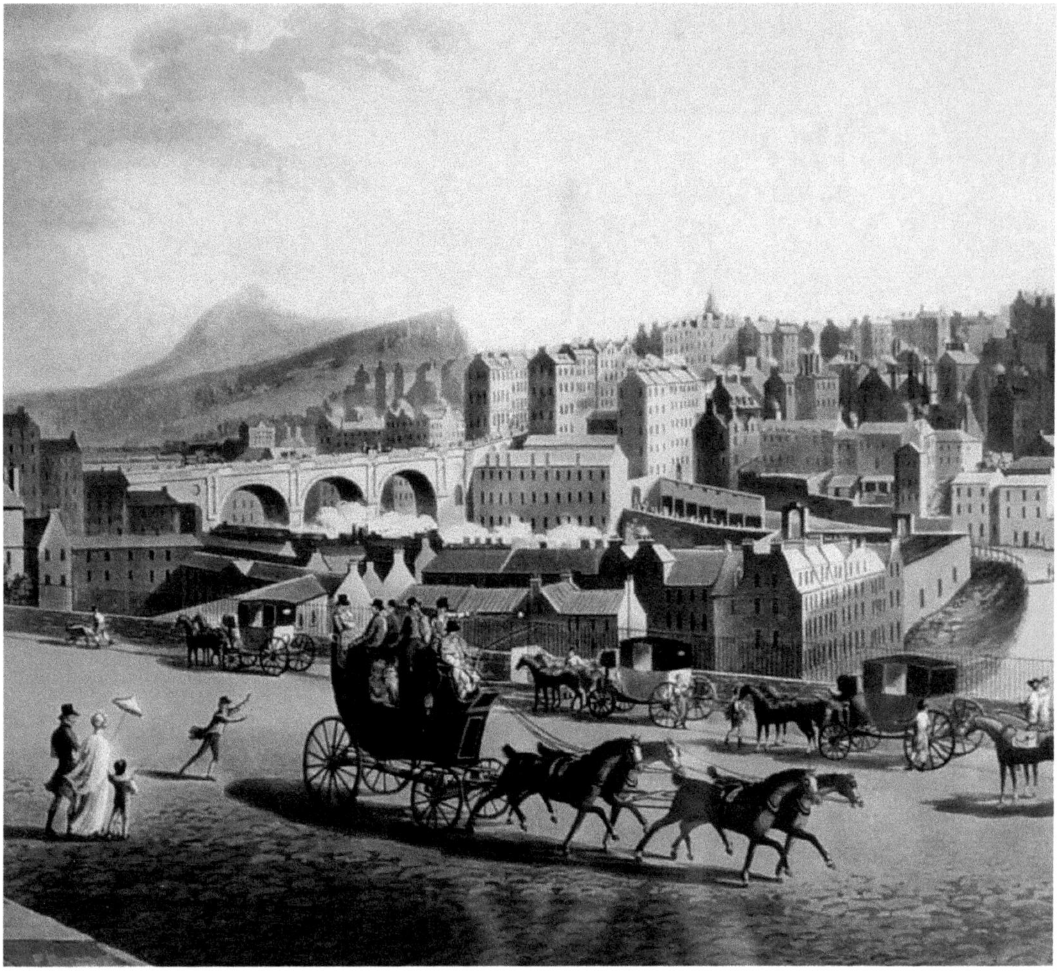

Carriages in Princes Street, *c.* 1814.

old town, although this opened owners to the risk of their horses disappearing. In 1772, the architect James Brown advertised for the return of his strayed or stolen Scotch Galloway horse that he kept in Ross Park on the south side of the Old Town. Although horse theft was punishable by hanging in the eighteenth century it was a not infrequent crime.

One of the best-known inns at the time was the Red Lion Inn, owned by Peter Ramsay and situated at the foot of St Mary's Wynd on the Cowgate. His 1751 advertisement focuses more on the horses' accommodation than that for their owners:

> The Red Lion Inn is now fitted up in the latest and most commodious manner for the reception of noblemen, gentlemen and others, their servants and horses, having the yard and coach-house well paved, the well and pond in good order, the stables handsomely done up, with new stalls properly divided, and sash windows in each stable, situated in such order as to prevent cold in the winter and too much heat in the summer seasons.

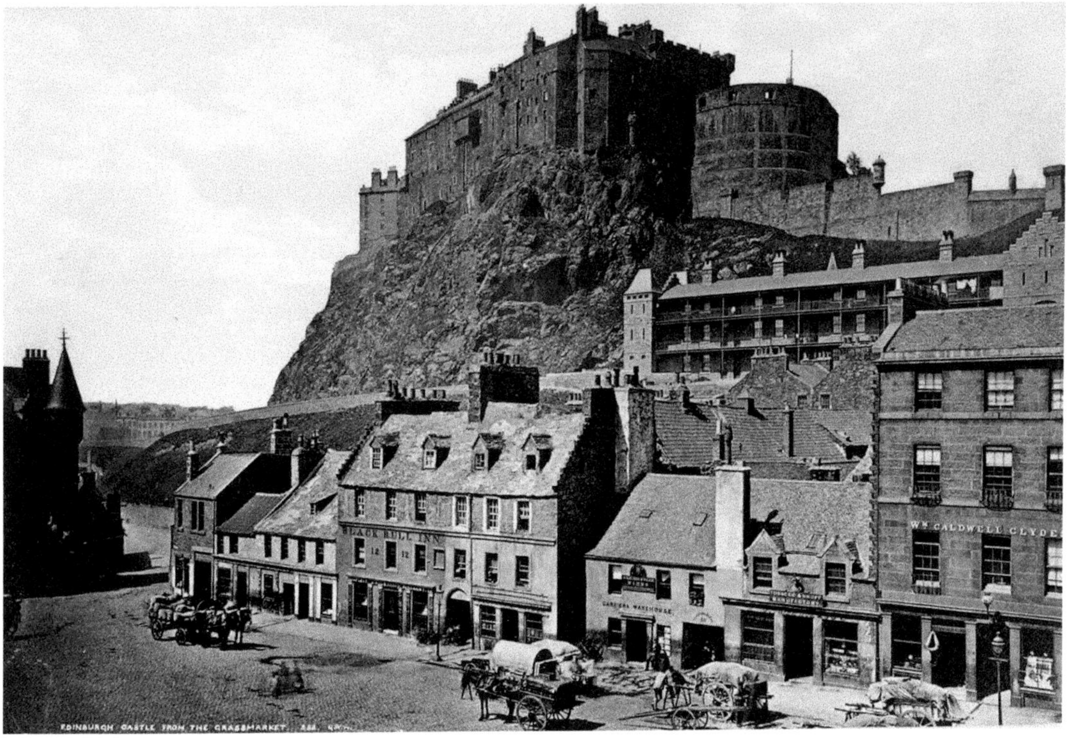

Grassmarket with Black Bull Inn, *c.* 1870.

Horses were raced on the sands at Leith before the races moved to Musselburgh in 1816. There is a record of a payment from James IV in 1504 to a young jockey who 'ran the King's horse' at Leith. The prizes were substantial. In July 1765 Mad Tom, a horse owned by a farrier in Haddington, won 30 guineas (equivalent to £4,000 today). The Leith Races were held for four or five days in the summer and were one of Edinburgh's great working-class festivals, with the sands crowded with booths and sideshows. The other popular horseback sport among the better-off was hunting, and in medieval times Scotland's royalty hunted deer in the woods around the city. However, by 1500 deer had almost disappeared from Holyrood Deer Park and from then on those who hunted near Edinburgh pursued foxes.

Although no one needed to take a test to ride a horse, it was important to ensure the horse was properly broken-in and that riders understood their mount's mood. Horses respond strongly to other horses and communicate through body language, and riders understanding these signals could save themselves an unforeseen movement that might unseat them. In 1761, a proposal for an Edinburgh riding school was advertised in the *Caledonian Mercury*:

> There is to be a meeting at the house of Mrs Walker, a vintner, for concerting the most proper plan of establishing a Riding School and an Academy for Exercises in Edinburgh. Some progress has already been made towards the success of it, and it is hoped that such noblemen and gentlemen as wish to promote this useful addition will attend the meeting at the time appointed.

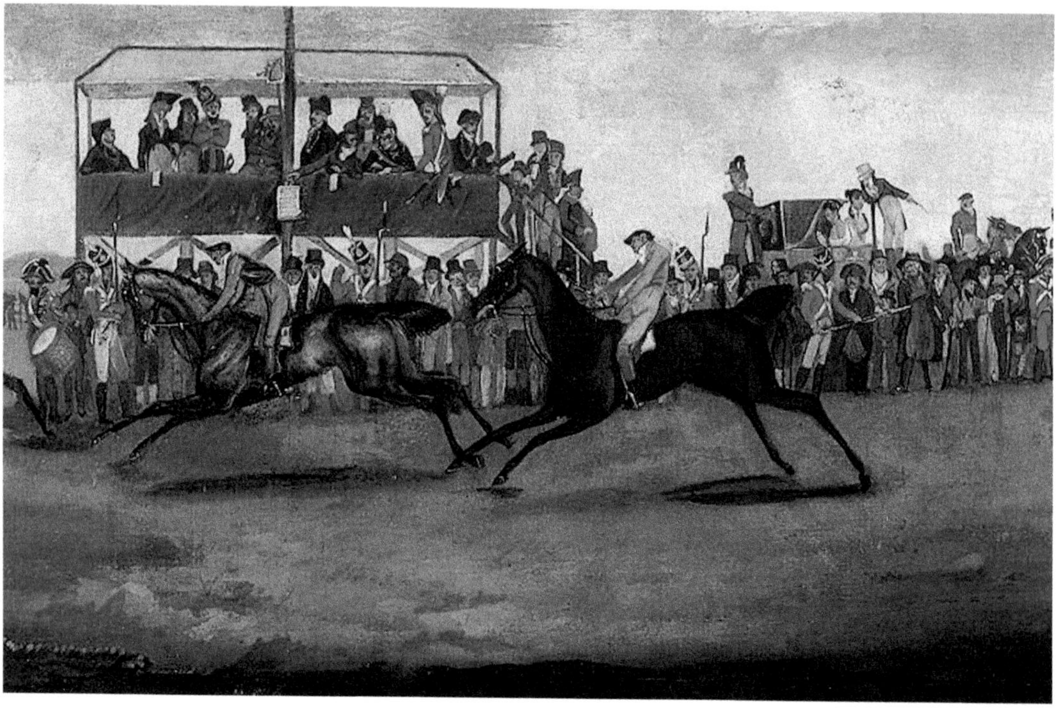

Detail from *Last of the Leith Races* by James Howe (1780–1836).

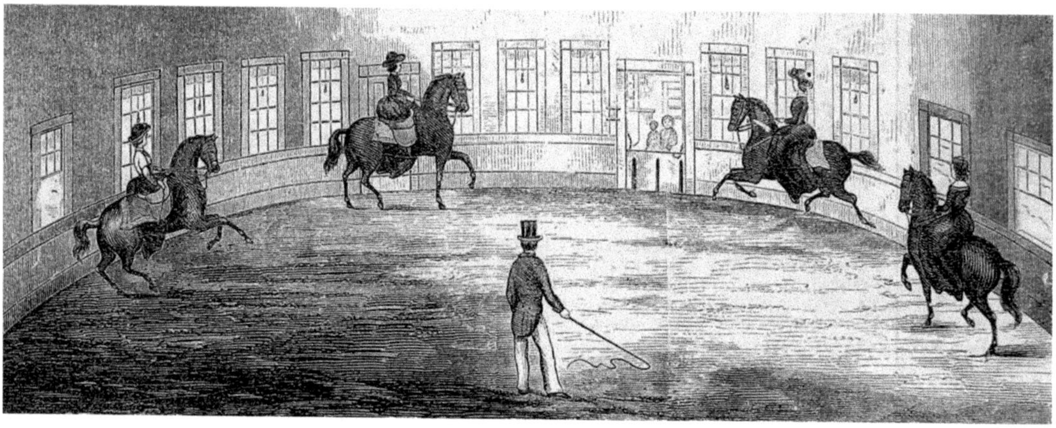

Female equestrians in a riding school *c.* 1800.

Designed by Robert Adam, the Royal Academy riding school opened in Nicolson Street in April 1764, and offered classes in horse-riding skills and the breaking-in of saddle horses. The government agreed to fund the post of riding master and an Italian, Angelo Tremamondo, was appointed in 1768. As well as equestrian, instruction the riding school held regular 'carousals'. These were displays of showy riding that proved popular with the fashionable set and often lasted for several days.

This day, a carousal at which a numerous and genteel company were preferred, was held at the Riding School. They rode with a care, gracefulness, and alertness and performed their exercises with great dexterity. A gold medal, given by Mr Angelo, was presented by the Countess of Selkirk to Robert Cay, of Northumberland as the prize of successful merit.

In 1793, in response to fears of a French invasion, Piershill Barracks was built on the eastern edge of the city to house cavalry regiments. Among the regiments stationed there was the Royal Regiment of Scots Dragoons. Formed in 1681, the regiment became known as the Scots Greys as the men rode grey horses, all of which had to be around 15.3 hands in height (5 ft 3 ins) and capable of supporting at least 17 stone in weight. The importance of the horse in war at this time is shown by the newspaper reports of the Scots Greys' casualties during the Battle of Waterloo in 1815: 'men killed – 20; horses killed or missing – 54; men wounded – 56; horses wounded – 14.'

The expansion of the city from the late eighteenth century boosted horse ownership and increased demand for the many related trades: saddlers, harness makers, grooms, fodder suppliers, horse trainers, farriers, horse dealers and blacksmiths. 'Horses fetched very high prices; there were a great many buyers, and such horses as could have been bought two or three years ago at £30 to £35 now fetched from £40 to £50 and even £60 was asked for several.' The increased number of horses on the roads led to Edinburgh introducing a series of regulations in 1808, one being a fine of 10s for 'any person who shall ride a horse furiously or improperly'. The great majority of saddle horses and carriage horses owned by individuals would have been well looked after, as they were

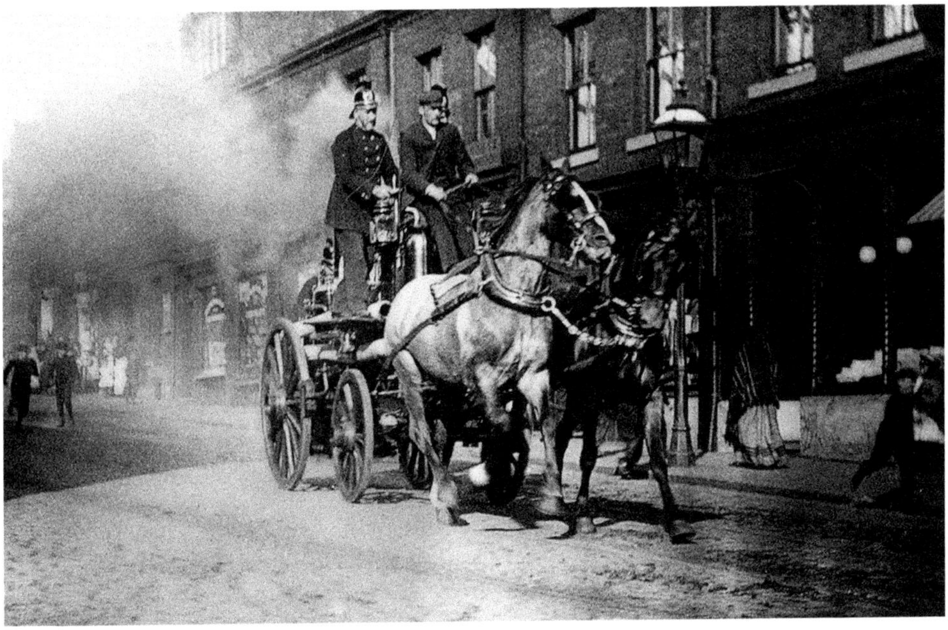

Horse-drawn fire engine, 1895.

an expensive investment and thus had a reasonable life. However, conditions for almost all the horses that hauled carts were harsh. When James V returned from France in 1537 with his new wife, Madeleine, the King of France's daughter, he sailed into Leith. On the king's ships were gun carriages and artillery equipment that had to be taken up to the castle. Around 130 trips were made by teams of four horses, all having to haul their loads the 3 miles and the 1,000 feet rise from Leith port to Edinburgh Castle.

Arduous exertion of this kind was common. To create the grand buildings and striking townhouses of the New Town, vast armies of horses were used to ferry the stone from Craigleith and the other quarries on the outskirts to the city's building sites, while other horses towed carts heavy with timber, slates and other building materials. All pulled their loads over mainly unmade narrow roads and lanes, and in all weathers. Thus, life expectancy for many of these cart horses was as low as three years. Around 1820 the great Clydesdale horse was bred for its strength and became particularly used in hauling heavy loads, but even such a strong horse might only last nine years given the relentless work expected of it.

Many of the New Town houses were built with a coach house and stables, and carriage ownership grew. Also, the city's expansion led to many more commercial horse-drawn vehicles, including small carts and vans delivering goods to local shops and houses,

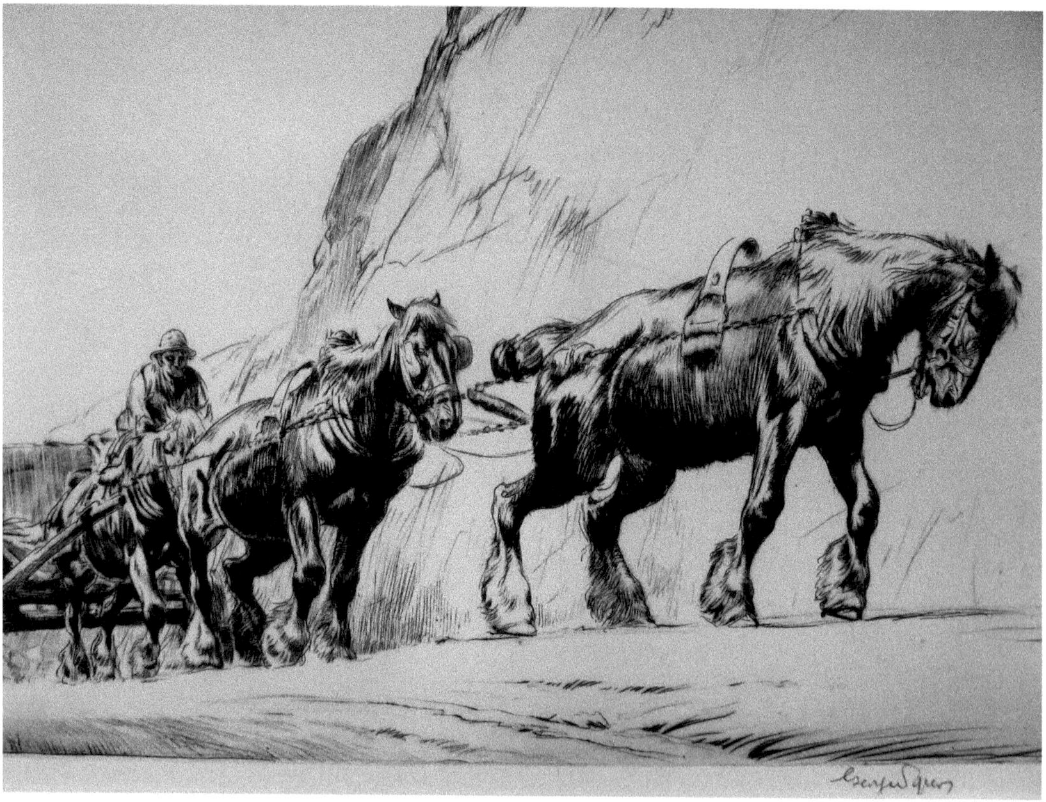

The Quarry Team by George Soper, 1922.

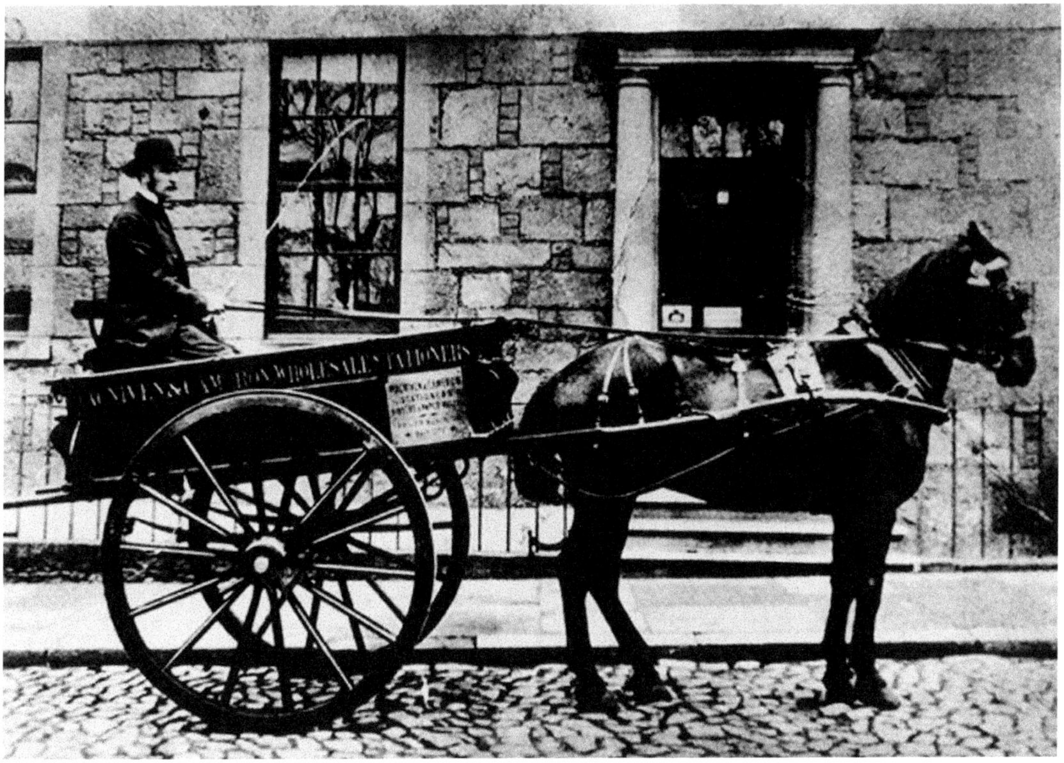

Delivery cart in George Square, *c.* 1900.

wagons ferrying coal, funeral coaches, fire engines, etc. While the majority of drivers would have treated their animals well, there were many instances of horses being forced to pull overloaded carts. This was a particular issue given Edinburgh's steep ascents, as a letter to *The Scotsman* in 1877 indicates: 'It was piteous to see the poor animals struggling up the steep incline from Waverley Bridge this morning – one driver was, as I passed, wiping the blood from the knees of one that had evidently fallen in the attempt.' Another letter writer described a horse being beaten by a stick for ten minutes to try to force the poor animal to set off with its excessive load. Only a few cart drivers were charged with cruelty, and these just in extreme circumstances. Many more men appeared in court charged with being drunk while in charge of horses, and when this led to an accident it was usually the horses that came off worse.

While some men might have thought owning a carriage an unnecessary expense, their wives probably argued otherwise. While women did ride saddle horses, this would have been difficult for the many young wives who spent the first decade or more of their marriage pregnant or recovering from childbirth, as very large families were the norm. For such women a family carriage offered the opportunity to travel to relations and friends. These carriages mainly were two-person vehicles pulled by one or two horses. Larger enclosed coaches drawn by two or four horses were owned by the wealthier residents.

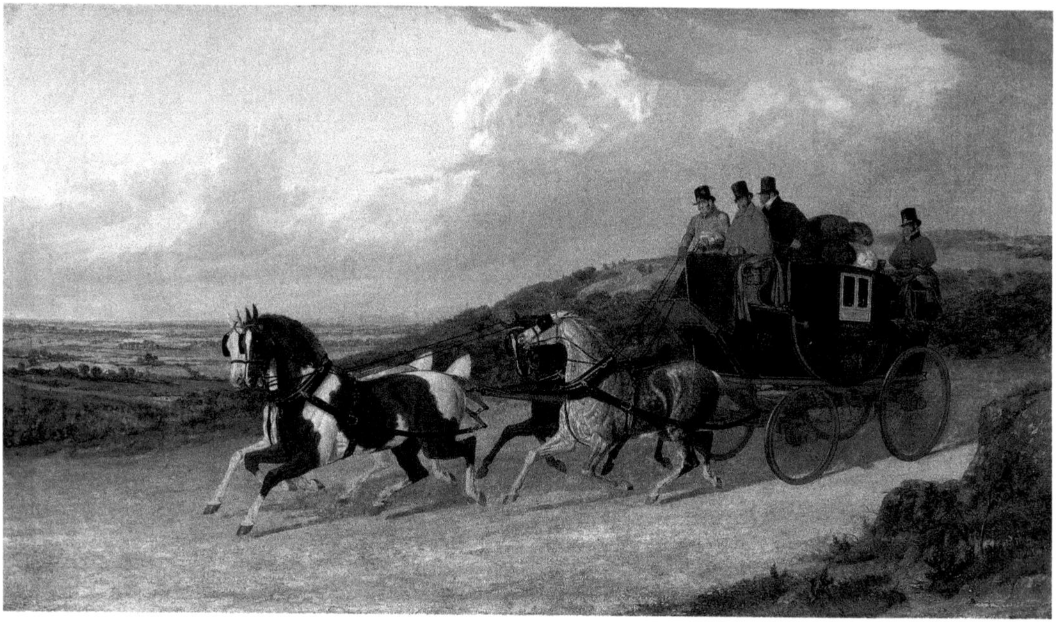

The Edinburgh and London Mail Stagecoach by John Frederick Herring (1795–1865).

The first public coach service in Scotland was introduced in 1610 and ran from Edinburgh to Leith until at least the 1730s. John Taylor, a poet wrote in 1623: 'A coach was a strange monster in those days and the sight of them put both horse and man to amazement. The mischiefs that hath been done by them are not to be numbered, as breaking of legs and arms, overthrowing down hills, over bridges, running over children, lame and old people.' Stagecoaches ran between Edinburgh and London from around 1658, although regular services did not become common until the early eighteenth century. One service in 1712 advertised that it would 'perform the whole journey in thirteen days without any stoppages (if God permits), having eighty able horses to perform the whole journey'. Another in 1752 advertised that the coach could carry four passengers at five guineas per passenger, each of whom was allowed 20 lb of luggage and charged 6*d* per lb for extra. In 1808, it was recorded that the weight of mail coaches that were pulled by four horses was 2,000 kilograms (2 tons) made up of the coach, four inside passengers, four outside passengers, a coachman, guard, mail and luggage.

Within the city the first hackney carriages began plying their trade in the 1670s and in the 1830s horse-drawn omnibuses began to operate. Forty years later horse-drawn trams were introduced. These were pulled by two horses, although on some of the steep hills five horses were needed to pull the weighty trams and those that were too steep even for multiple horsepower were pulled up by a steam-powered cable system. The increased use of horses in the city caused concern. In 1894, *The Times* called the situation 'The Great Horse Manure Crisis' and predicted that in fifty years every street in London would be buried under 9 feet of manure.

By the Second World War few horses were to be seen on the city's streets, although some horse-drawn vehicles continued into the 1950s, and milk carts even later. The recreational use of horses continued and thrives today, although the situation is similar to that written about in 1946: 'Riding is financially beyond the means of many as a pastime, and good horses are hard to come by.'

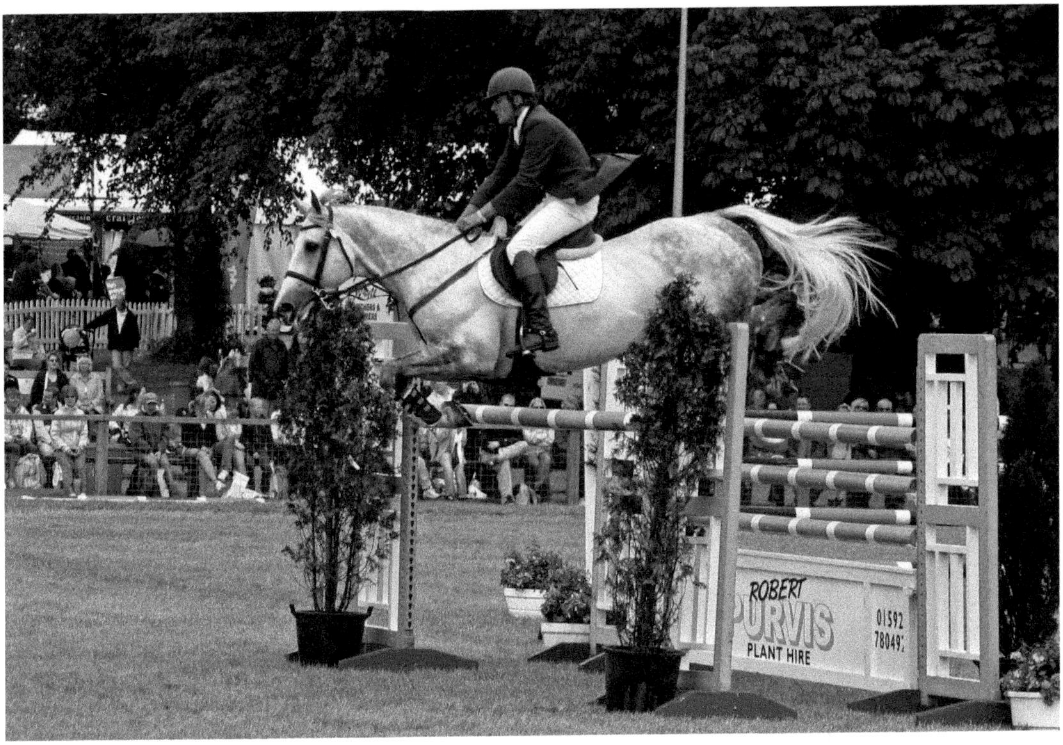

Showjumping at the 2008 Royal Highland Show, Edinburgh. (Photo courtesy of Edinburgh Blog)

2. Equestrian Performances

In the mid-eighteenth century, equestrian shows became popular and as Edinburgh's cramped, overcrowded medieval old town lacked space for such displays, these were staged outside the town. In 1765, one took place in Comely Gardens behind Holyrood Abbey and featured Joseph Faulks, who performed 'several surprising exploits, including riding a horse while standing with his feet on top of the saddle and playing on the French horn'.

In 1768, Philip and Patty Astley established Astley's Riding School in London, and there Philip taught horsemanship in the morning and performed equestrian tricks in the afternoon. That same year Philip introduced a clown act in a short play called *Tailor's Ride to Brentford* and so is often credited as the 'father of modern circus', although it was his rival, Charles Dibdin, who first used the term 'circus' for dramatic equestrian entertainments by naming his London venue, the Royal Circus.

The development of the New Town offered space for new buildings and in March 1786 James and George Jones advertised for subscribers for an equestrian venue similar to Astley's in London. The Jones brothers ran an Equestrian Amphitheatre in London's Whitechapel and their proposal was to create 'an Edinburgh Circus: an Amphitheatre for Exercise and Amusement'. Their advert played to Edinburgh's pride:

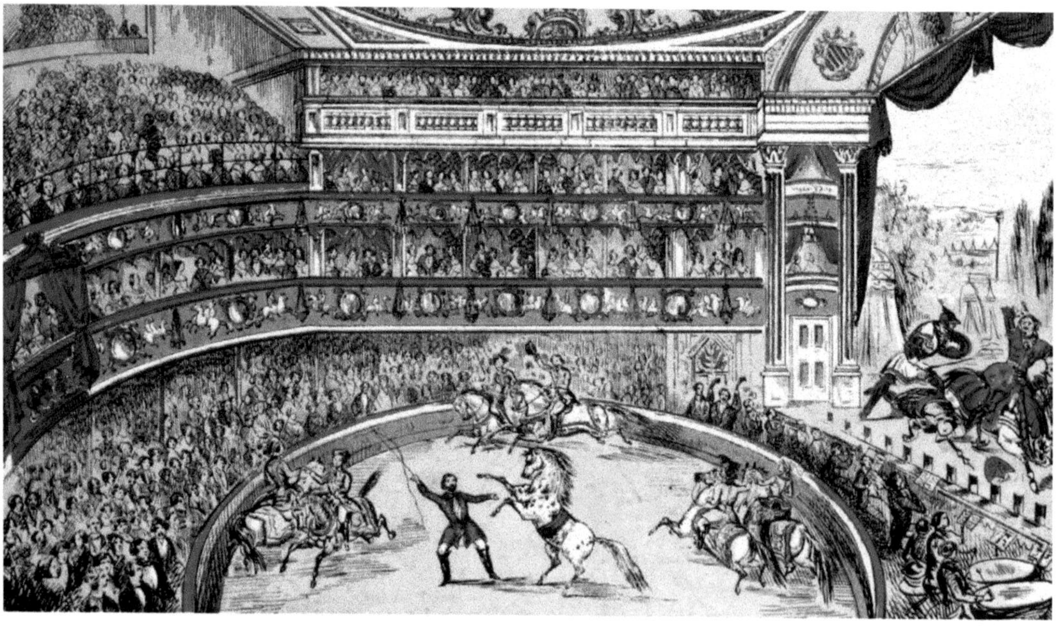

Astley's Equestrian Theatre in London.

> The metropolis of this ancient kingdom has maintained and established her right to be the second city of Great Britain, in magnitude, in numbered inhabitants, politeness, accommodation and amusement. The chief inducements which formerly led people of condition to London now operate in favour of Edinburgh; and there are but a few things remaining either of curiosity or entertainment, which can determine them to prefer the former. One entertainment, indeed, is yet wanting, equally calculated to answer the purpose of exercise of diversion, an entertainment which brings strangers in crowds to London. Every person who has visited the capital of Great Britain is acquainted with the assemblage of entertainments afforded by the Royal Circus and Astley's Amphitheatre. These are superb buildings, containing under the same roof, practical riding schools, together with elegant theatres, in which are seen all the feats of strength and activity, with music, and those lighter entertainments of the stage, for which Sadler's Wells has been long famous. We most respectfully lay the following proposal before the public that we shall immediately erect a Circus at Edinburgh, upon the very same plan with those in London.

To stimulate interest and encourage financial subscribers, in 1786 the brothers brought to Edinburgh a company of nine equestrian performers led by an accomplished horseman, William Parker, and they performed at the Circular Riding School in Dr Hope's Park

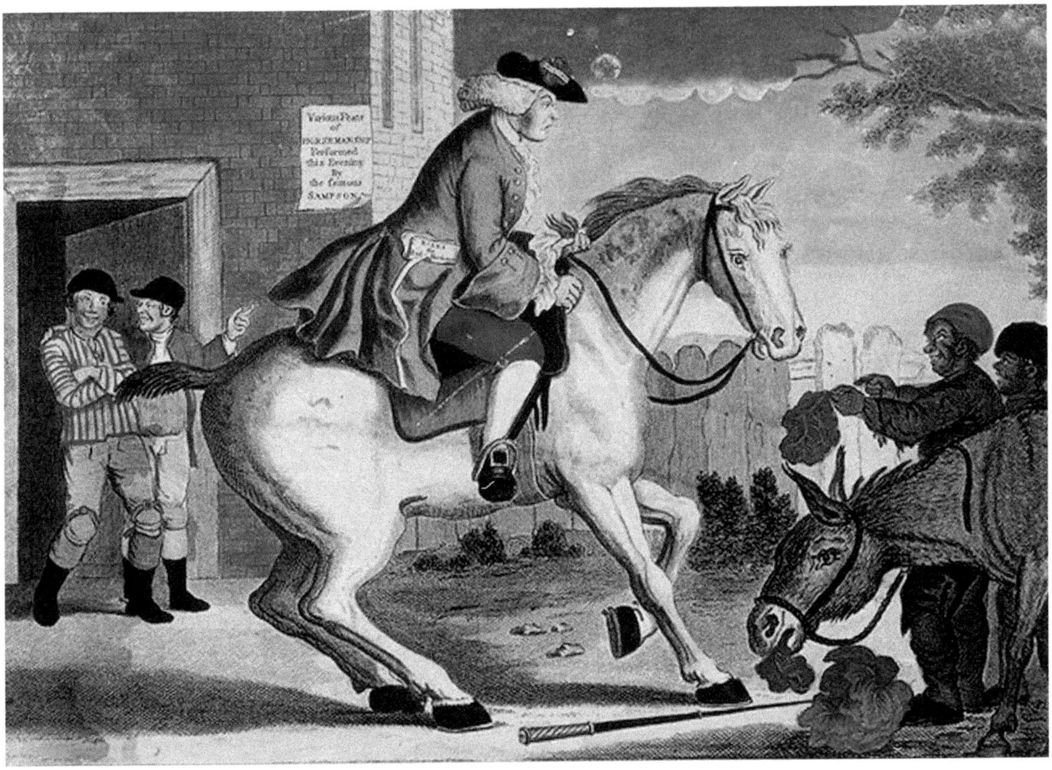

Scene from *The Tailor Rides to Brentford* by John Collett, *c.* 1770.

in Leith Walk. The brothers also mounted a version of Astley's popular *Tailor's Ride to Brentford* and further equestrian shows over the following three years.

In January 1790, the Edinburgh Equestrian Circus opened on a site in King Street (now the site of the hall of St Mary's Catholic Cathedral), and the *Scots Magazine* reviewed the opening night:

> The Edinburgh Equestrian Circus opened on Monday with a variety of entertainments. The company who attended the Circus were no less brilliant than numerous. Mr Parker's great abilities in the Equestrian Exercises were fully displayed on the occasion and most deservedly applauded. Messrs Sutton, King, and Ricketts, in their various and repeated exertions to please, did not lose their share of merit, and received the gratification of the audience in numerous claps; as did Mr Jenkinson, whose abilities as the clown in the horsemanship excited the laughter of every one present. The Ground and Lofty Tumbling, if not superior, was at least equal, to any performance of the kind ever exhibited.

Also included in the opening evening were rope dancing and a ballet, *The Caledonian Shepherds.* In spite of its glittering opening the Edinburgh Equestrian Circus closed after just three years. One of its principal equestrian performers, John Bill Ricketts, left for

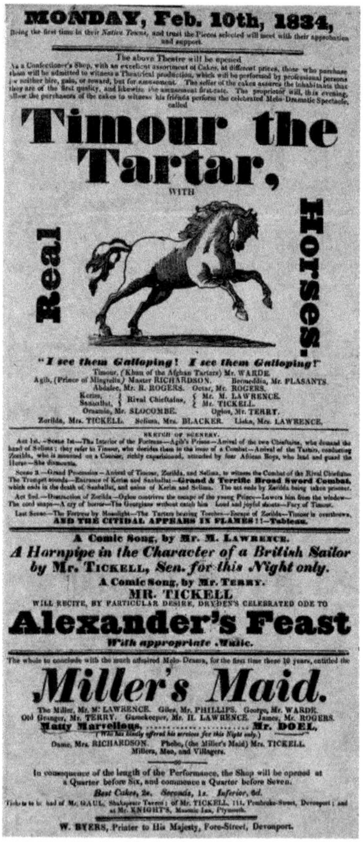

Poster advertising Timour the Tartar (1834).

America. He set up his own circus in Philadelphia and is generally credited as the founder of American circus. In 1817, the venue was taken over by Mr Corri and horses were back on the stage for the opening show, *The Grand Equestrian Burletta Spectacle of Timour, Khan of the Tartars!* There was a fashion for shows that included live horses and performers on stage recreating scenes, many featuring battles. Later that year the theatre featured:

> A grand entré of beautiful stud horses. By word of command the horses lie down and sit up, and take other truly astonishing positions. Mr Clark is the most dashing rider that has ever been in Scotland; and added to this, his tricks with oranges and old forks, marbles and bottle, are such that he may fairly claim rivalship with the Indian Jugglers.

A year later, *The Grand Equestrian Harlequinade, called The High Mettled Racer* was performed. *Chambers's Edinburgh Journal* described the plot:

> The horse appeared in the first scene as a racer, in all the life and vigour common to that high-bred animal, impatient of the rein, and champing on the bit till he started. In the next scene he appeared as a hunter, expressing his eagerness by pawing the ground, erecting his

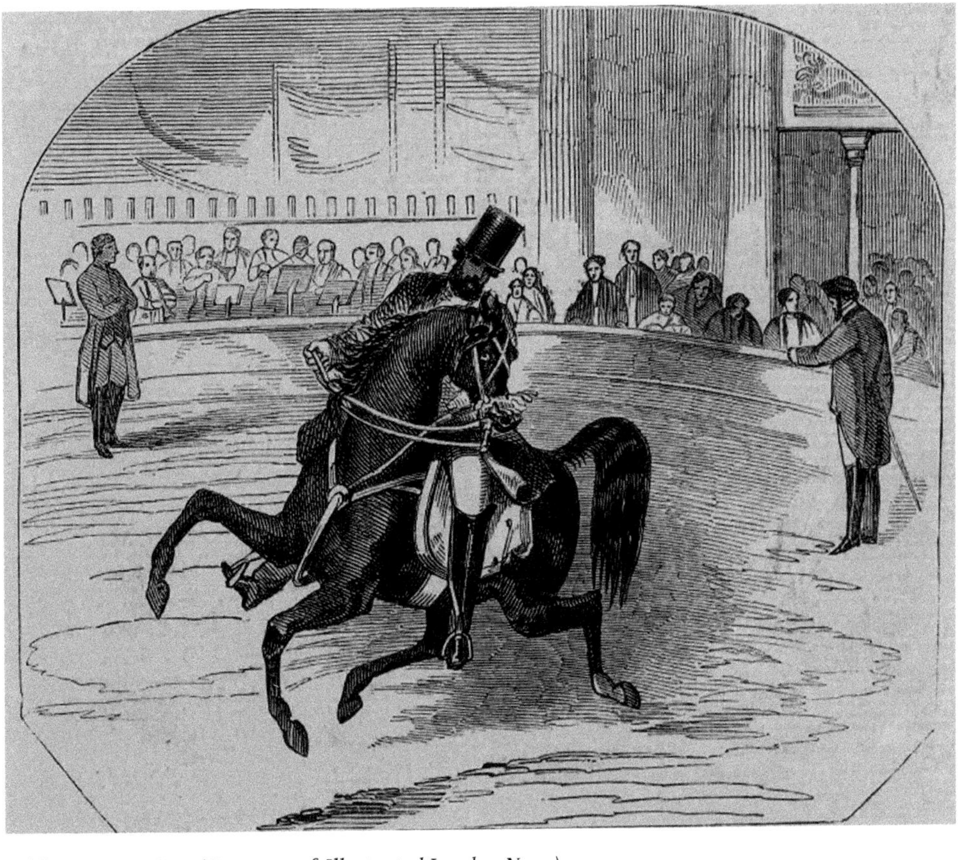

Pablo Fanque, 1847. (Courtesy of *Illustrated London News*)

ears, and snorting, till he was off to the full cry of the hounds. (For this part a number of horses started from the very back of the theatre and charged, passing through the pit.) Next, he appeared in harness as a post-horse, aged and fatigued, standing with knees bent and lowered head and when mounted, he went out with all the truth of such a reduced state. He then appeared drawing a sand-cart, in a situation of positive decrepitude, with his head down, his lips dropped, enduring the seeming harsh treatment of an unfeeling master, till he finally dropped and died. You saw him stretched out with sharp angular projecting bones, parts of his hide galled, and his bare ribs boldly portrayed on his miserable sides. He lies thus, a most affecting spectacle to the pitying audience, and is about to be consigned to one of those men who purchase dying and dead horses for the sale of their skins. But, by a coup de theatre, the once high-mettle racer is happily saved from this conclusion to his career. A magician enters, and, after some amusing jugglery, raises the animal to life and vigour. His skin instantaneously assumes its original gloss, his sores disappear, his bones cease to be visible, and he gallops off the stage amidst the plaudits of a thousand hands.

In 1851, the renowned equestrian performer Pablo Fanque created a new pantomime, *Harlequin Tam o' Shanter and his Mare Meg* although Robert Burns might have objected to Fanque interspersing 'fairy scenes which have a very gorgeous effect, and are much

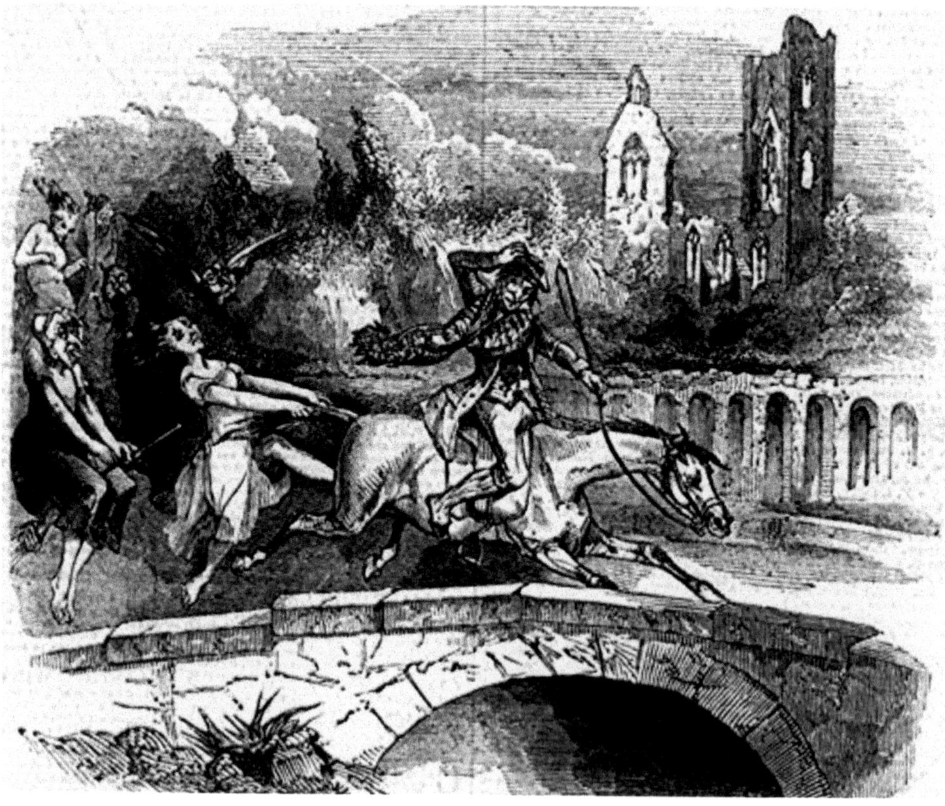

Scene from *Harlequin Tam o' Shanter and His Mare Meg*, 1844. (Courtesy of *Illustrated London News*)

heightened with some tableaux formed by milk-white steeds, richly caparisoned, and attended by the goddesses of poetry and music, and a brilliant train of elfin sprites' into the middle of the scene showing the witches dancing to 'hornpipes, jigs, strathspeys, and reels'.

However, given Shakespeare's famous line 'A horse, a horse, my kingdom for a horse', the playwright might have been quite taken by William Cooke's touring equestrian circus performance in Edinburgh in 1854:

> The concluding part of the programme was the last act of Richard the Third. The novelty of horses assisting the performance of a Shakespearian tragedy caused the piece to go off with great enthusiasm, and indeed, considering the disadvantages of the occasion, among others the total absence of scenery, the affair was acted creditably.

Edward Dutton Cook, a Victorian theatre critic, would have been pleased to have seen the horse given a part in this classic drama for in *A Book Of The Play – Studies and Illustrations of Histrionic Story, Life, and Character* he lamented the loss of opportunities for four-legged performers, as by this time most equestrian circuses had begun to evolve into the modern circus format that included other animals, such as lions and monkeys, and tightrope walkers and acrobats:

> The circus flourishes, and quadrupeds figure now and then upon the stage, but the "horse spectacle" has almost vanished. The noble animal is to be seen occasionally on the boards, but he is cast for small parts only, is little better than a four-footed supernumerary.

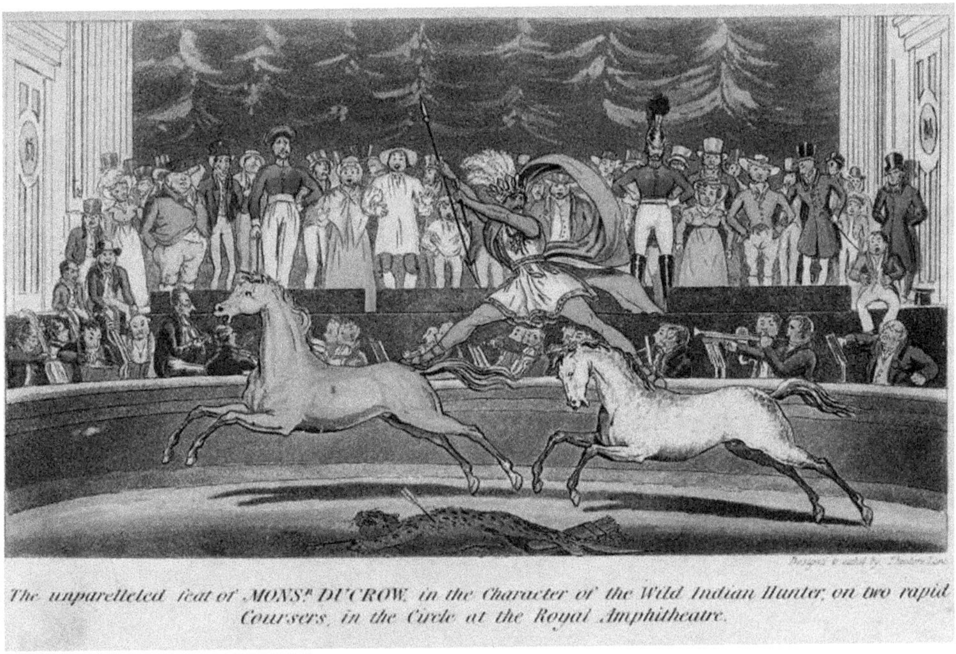

Andrew Ducrow, 'The Colossus of equestrians', in the Royal Amphitheatre, *c.* 1830.

> He comes on to aid the pageantry of the scene; Plays are not now written for him. He is no longer required to evince the fidelity and devotion of his nature by knocking at street-doors, rescuing a prisoned master, defending oppressed innocence, or dying in the centre of the stage to slow music. Something of a part seemed promised him when the popular drama of Flying Scud was first represented; at least, he supplied that work with its title. But it was speedily to be perceived that animal interests had been subordinated to human. More prominent occupation by far was assigned to the rider than to the horse. A different plan of distributing parts prevailed when The High-mettled Racer and kindred works adorned the stage. A horse with histrionic instincts and acquirements had something like a chance then. But now he can only lament the decline of the equestrian drama. True, the circus is still open to him; but in the eyes of a well-educated performing horse a circus must be much what a music-hall is in the opinion of a tragedian devoted to five-act plays.

John Cooke took over his father's touring circus in the 1870s and in 1874 moved it to a permanent home in Edinburgh. It was housed in a large tent on Grindlay Street until 1882 when the building of the Royal Lyceum Theatre forced it to move to a new building,

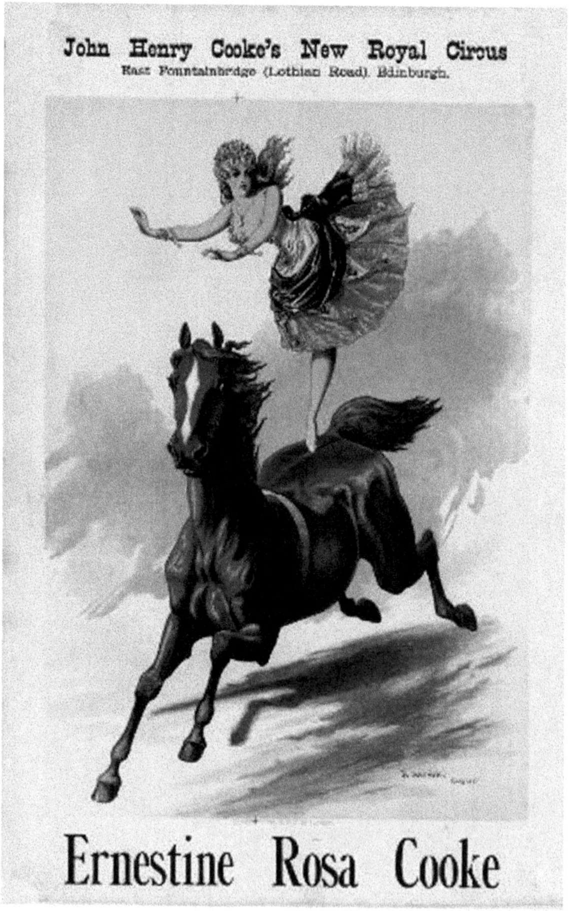

Poster for Cooke's Circus showing Ernestine Rosa Cooke, *c.* 1880.

the Royal Circus, in East Fountainbridge. Although clowns and other performers were included, equestrian acts remained the core of the shows and Cooke's four sons and two daughters all performed on horses. 'Ernestine Rosa Cooke excels in her equestrian performances and her grand finale with the trained doves was exceedingly pretty.' Cooke's Circus closed in 1910.

In 1904, *Buffalo Bill's Wild West & Congress of Rough Riders of the World* visited Edinburgh for a week and, with 500 horses taking part, surpassed any previous equestrian attraction. The show arrived in the city in three trains of forty-nine wagons and the performing tent that was erected in Gorgie accommodated at least 18,000 people; around 140,000 people saw the show during its week in Edinburgh. William Cody's extravaganza not only included cowboys and Native Americans, but also Cossacks, Arabs and members of the Imperial Japanese Cavalry.

> As the men and women of different nations rode into the arena mounted on exceptionally fine horses, they performed various acts of horsemanship which clearly indicated life-long experience in the saddle. Members of various tribes of North American Redskins, were the first to make their appearance. These were followed by Arabs, Japanese, Cossacks, American Artillerymen, Cowboys, lady-riders, English Lancers, and others, all of which were superbly mounted and handled their charges with

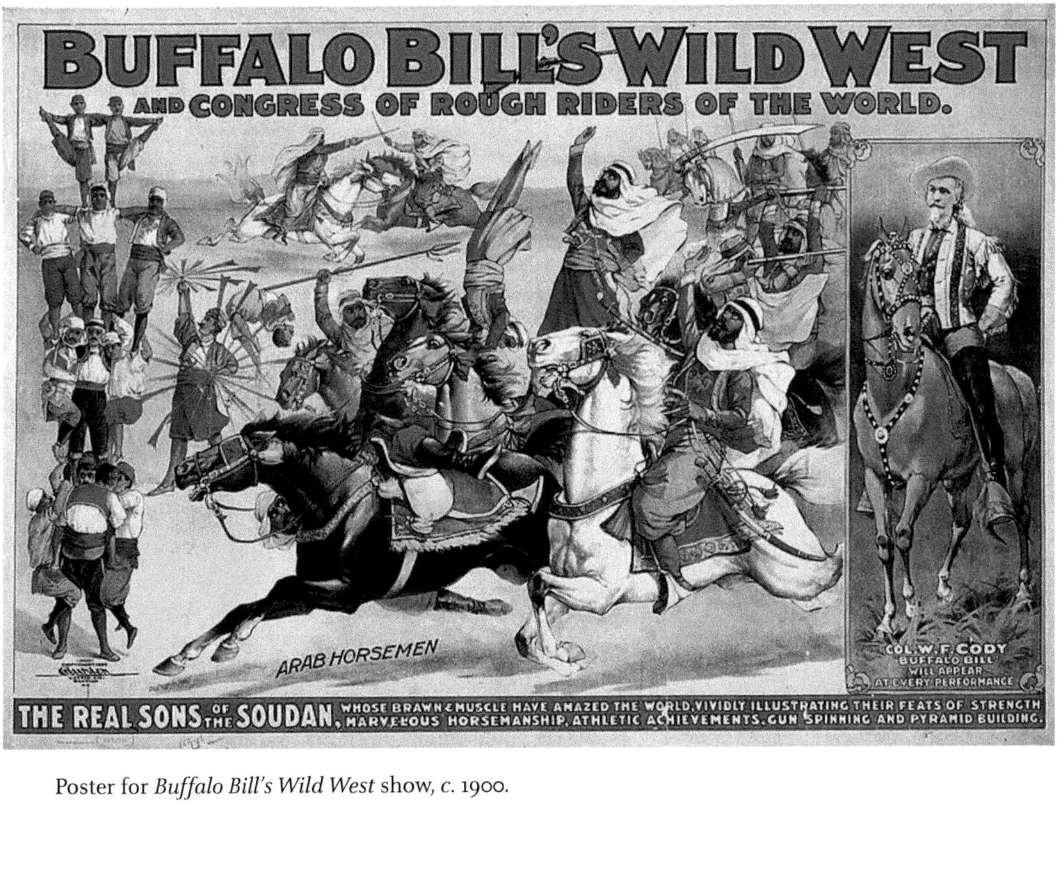

Poster for *Buffalo Bill's Wild West* show, *c.* 1900.

> great skill ... All over, the horsemanship was perfect, and besides exhibiting absolute control of the animals, many feats of an extraordinary nature were performed by the riders while moving at a terrific speed. The horsewomen were in no way inferior to the horsemen, displaying equally as much skill and even more gracefulness. A scene depicting a part of American history, known as 'Custer's Last Stand', was the occasion of much rushing about among the Indians and Americans, rifle firing, shouting, etc. and an attack on the 'Deadwood Mail' was not without interest.

Few opportunities for horses to tread the boards arise these days, but in 2015 one horse had the opportunity to play a unicorn in *The Enchanted Wintergarden*, a performance by Scotland's first Equestrian theatre group, Les Amis D'Onno. Appropriately, the play was performed at Summerhall, an arts venue in what was previously the Royal (Dick) School of Veterinary Studies.

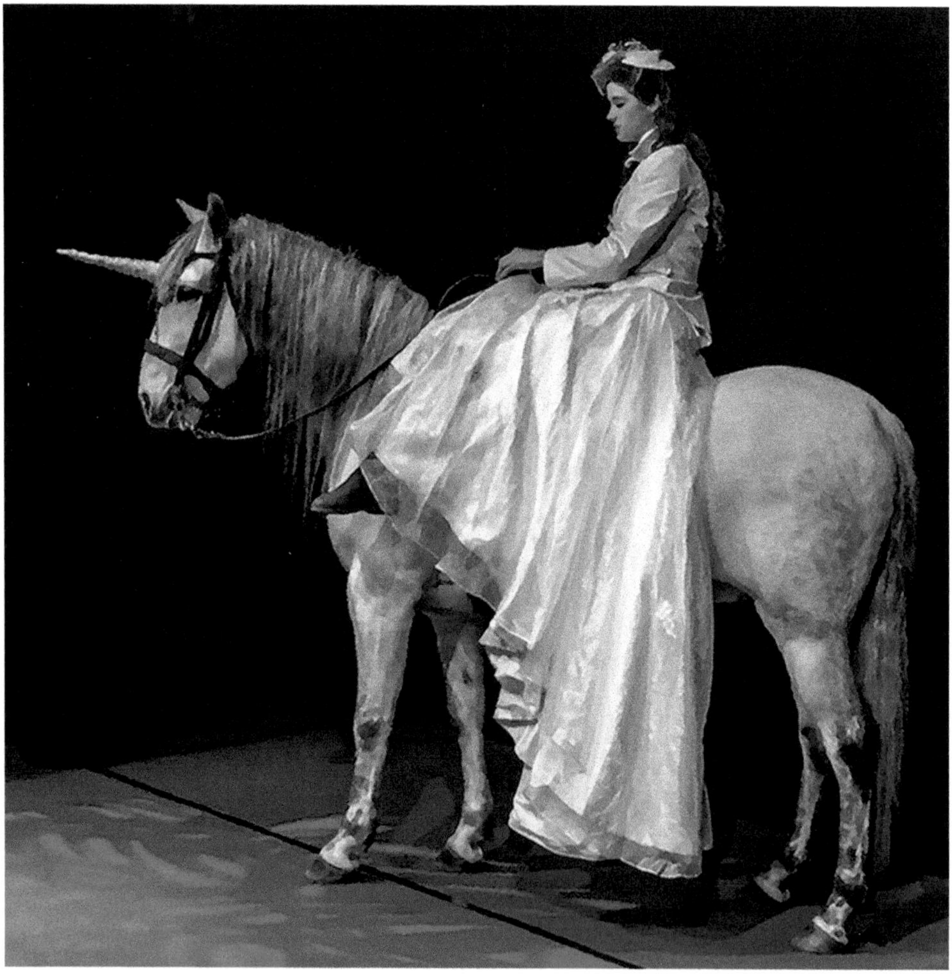

The Enchanted Wintergarden performed by Les Amis D'Onno, 2015. (Courtesy of Dougie Johnston)

3. Menageries

In 1506, a lion arrived at Leith docks for James IV. The lion was particularly prized by royalty as it was considered 'the king of beasts' and it had particular significance for James given the animal's place on the Scottish coat of arms. The lion was housed at Holyrood Palace and other animals were added to what became the king's menagerie, including a tiger, lynx and an ape, but the menagerie disappeared after the Union of the Crowns in 1603.

There was money to be made from exhibiting unfamiliar animals and a few reached Edinburgh. In 1659, John Nicholl recorded in his diary that 'thair wes brocht to this natioun ane heigh great beast, callit ane Drummodrary, quhilk being keipit clos in the Cannogait, nane hade a sight of it without thrie pence', and an elephant was displayed in 1705. In 1747, a menagerie, possibly the first to be publicly exhibited, was shown in George Ramsay's stables in Canongate, and included a 'rhinoceros or real unicorn',

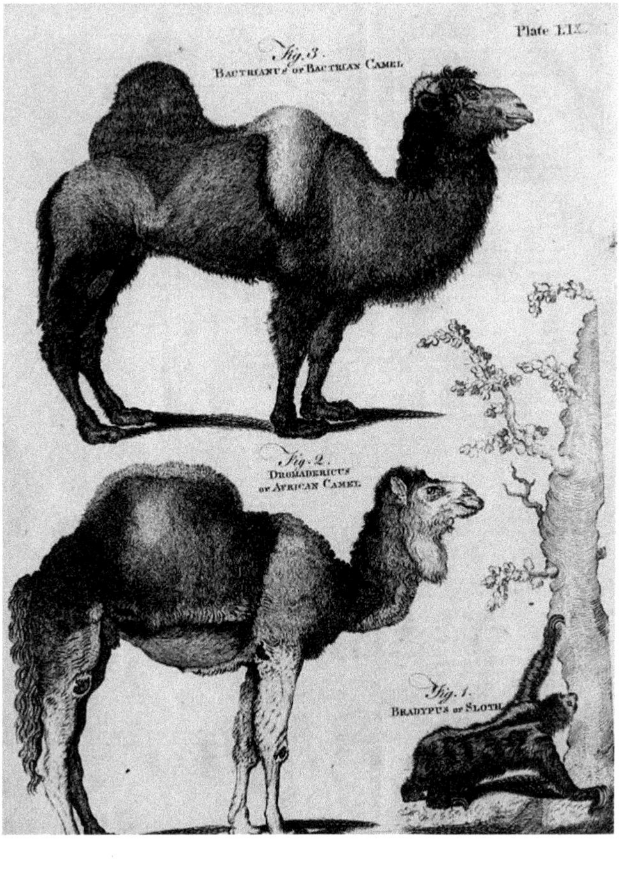

Bactrianus or Bactrian Camel from *Encyclopaedia Britannica Volume One* published in Edinburgh in 1768.

a buffalo, an ape and a 'man tiger or mountain monster'. In 1762, Christopher 'Pinchy' Pinchbeak brought his private menagerie to the city:

> To those who are endowed with the noble spirit of curiosity. To be seen at the Black Bull, a vast variety of natural productions, viz. The beautiful zebra (late Her Majesty's); a magnificent lion, remarkably lively, tame, and docile; a real Bengal Tyger, the largest ever seen in the memory of man; a young Oran-outang, that has a great resemblance of the human species; a miraculous Porcupine; a voracious Panther, a beautiful young Leopard; and many other animals equally curious. Price to the Nobility is left to their own generosity. Ladies and gentlemen one shilling.

The zebra had been given as a wedding gift to the new wife of George III and it was housed in the Tower of London. The public flocked to see it but not everyone was impressed. Henry Howard wrote a humorous bawdy song in which he referred to the zebra as 'the queen's ass'. Over time Londoners lost interest in the zebra and as it was costly to maintain it was sold to Pinchbeak, a clockmaker and friend of the king.

George Wombwell's menagerie first came to Edinburgh in 1820 and was erected on the 'Earthen Mound', the area behind the Royal Scottish Academy where the National Gallery of Scotland was later built. It included 'a Great Polar or Sea Monster', the first polar bear to be exhibited in the city. The surgeon and naturalist Francis Buckland described Wombwell's set-up:

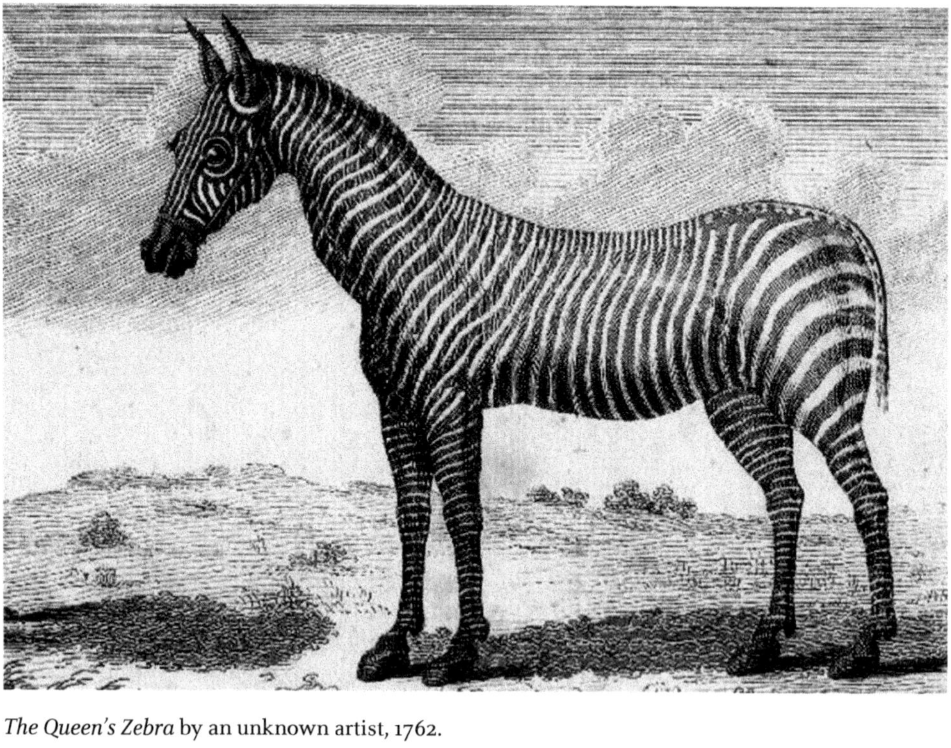

The Queen's Zebra by an unknown artist, 1762.

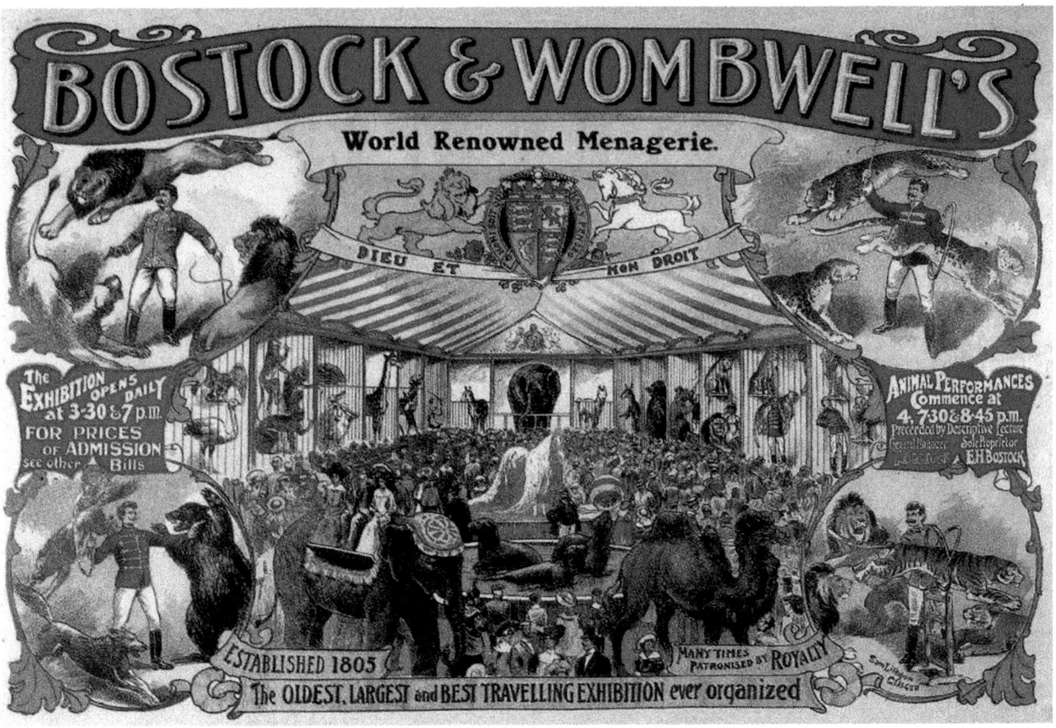

Poster for Wombwell's Royal Menagerie.

The establishment consists of fifteen vans and when they arrive on the exhibiting ground they are formed into two lines, with the long elephant van at one end, and the 'pay here' van at the other, the whole being roofed over with canvas. Between thirty and forty men are employed as keepers, and forty-five horses are attached to the establishment to drag the vans. Many of the keepers have 'apartments' in the vans behind the animals - one man having for his neighbour the hyenas; another the bear who 'rattles his chain all night'; another the lioness and her cubs which cry as loud and as continuously as any babies. All the animals are carried in the vans, except the two elephants; these intelligent beasts walk, but yet in such a manner that they shall not exhibit their huge cameos for nothing. Accordingly a van 27 feet long is provided, the bottom of which comes out, and the elephants march away famously, their huge feet only being exposed to the public; this acts as an advertisement, and makes the folks anxious to see the rest of their bodies. They can march twenty miles a day, but ten miles is about their usual day's journey. These elephants are wonderful performers. When not performing they stand like importunate beggars, thrusting their long trunks among the spectators for halfpence, which they immediately spend at a cake and nut stall within reach of their trunks; they place their money on the stall, and receive the eatables in return. When not served immediately, they ring a bell to call the attention of the black man who keeps the stall, and let him know they wish to make a purchase.

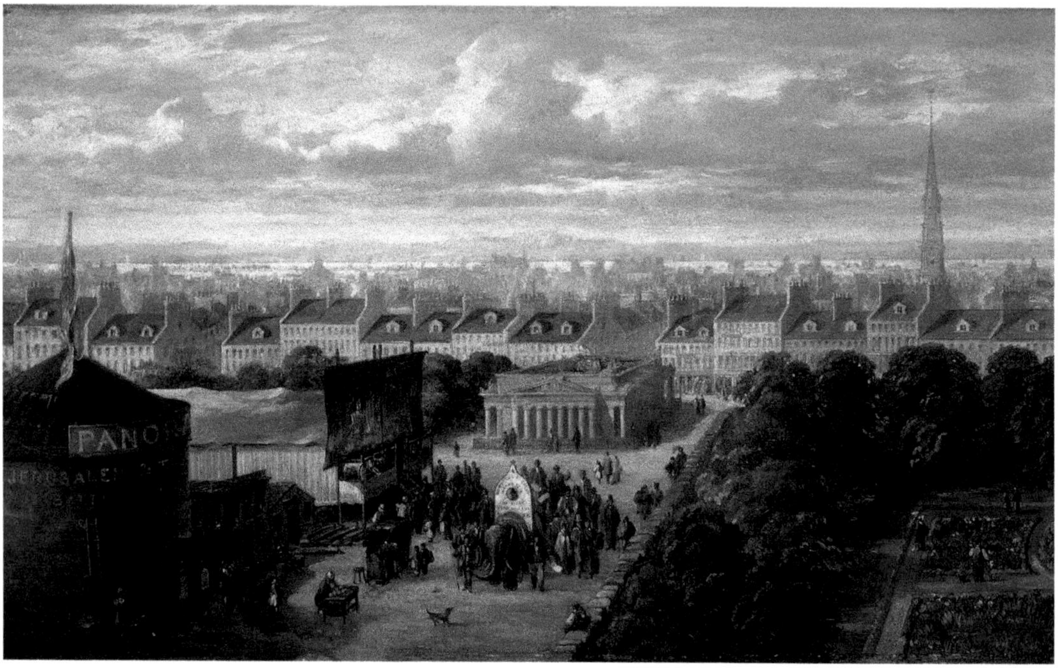

Wombwell's Menagerie on the Earthen Mound by Charles Halkerston, 1843. (Courtesy of City Art Centre, Edinburgh Museums and Galleries)

While in Edinburgh a lioness gave birth – the first African lion cub to be bred in Britain – and Wombwell named the cub Wallace in honour of Scotland's great hero. In *The Old Showmen and the Old London Fairs*, Thomas Frost described the day in 1825 when the grown-up Wallace lived up to his legendary courageous namesake:

> Some gentlemen in Warwick who possessed several celebrated bull-dogs which had distinguished themselves in bullbaiting, offered to wager that their dogs could successfully fight a lion. Mr Wombwell accepted the wager, and the dogs were sent into the den with a lion called Nero. This animal was very tame, and indeed so lamb-like in temper was he that the public were allowed, on payment of twopence, to enter his den and get a ride on his back – a privilege of which large numbers daily took advantage. Well Nero, when he saw the bull-dogs enter his den, slunk away to a corner, and would not be tempted to fight. The dogs were then drawn and placed in the den of a second lion, called Wallace. In this lion the dogs found a different customer to deal with, and in a short time the six famed bulldogs were successively killed.

Two years later a man 'imprudently and incautiously' placed his hand through the bars of Wallace's cage and the lion seized the man's arm with his teeth. Luckily, the keeper saved the man from serious injury. The incident was embellished by Marriott Edgar in his humorous poem 'The Lion and Albert', in which a young boy decides to prod the dozing lion with a stick. It ends:

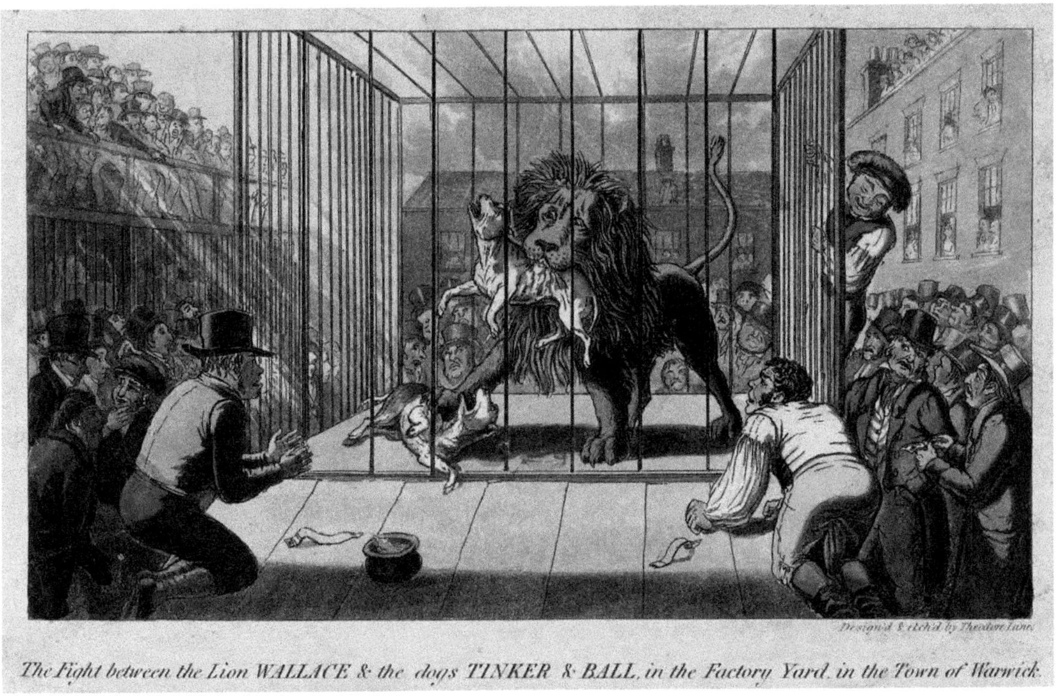

The fight between the lion Wallace and the dogs Tinker and Ball by Theodore Lane, 1825.

> You could see that the Lion didn't like it,
> For giving a kind of a roll,
> He pulled Albert inside the cage with 'im,
> And swallowed the little lad 'ole.

The sight of unusual animals often upset horses and dogs. In 1824, a kangaroo that was being exhibited was attacked by a dog and had part of its nose bitten off. The dog's owner was fined a guinea. While viewing the animals was popular, what people most wanted to see were the lion tamers and Sir Gerrard Tyrwhitt-Drake described George Wombwell's lion taming in *English Fairs and Circuses*:

> Captain Wombwell was a heavily built man, about 5ft. 8 in. in height, with fair hair, a long waxed moustache, and the largest hands I ever saw. He was attired in a crimson plush jacket with gold braiding and frogs – evidently made before he became so stout, as it would not meet anywhere. It was emblazoned with many medals presented to him to record special deeds of valour – in the menagerie and not on the battlefield. Armed only with a twisted willow whip stock and rawhide thong, he would climb slowly up the steps leading to the door of the cage. With his hands on the door-catch and his eye on the position of the animals, he would at the right moment open the door, and with extraordinary agility for such a heavy man, be inside with the door slammed behind him in a split second. Then the fun began. The five big lions would start bounding round

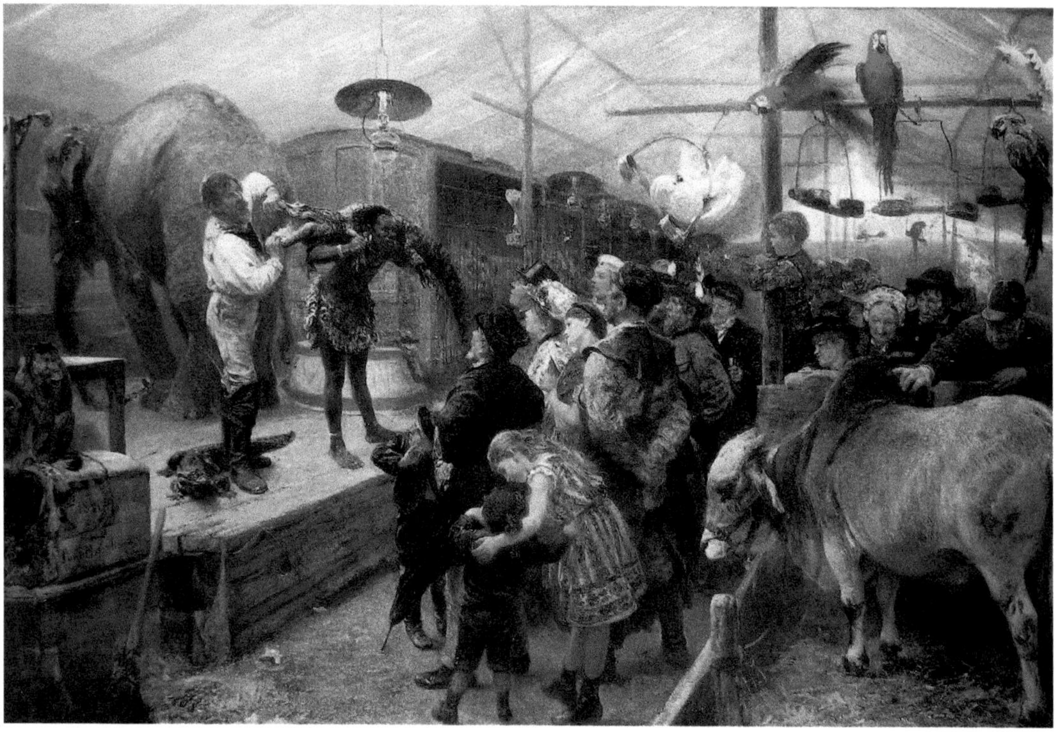

'A travelling menagerie' by Paul Meyerheim, 1894.

> the 6ft-wide cage, with Wombwell unconcernedly standing in the centre. After the first mad rush round, the usual jumping and posing took place and then, to my mind, the most exciting moment arrived when the trainer had to leave the cage. Again, the exact moment had to be gauged for a hasty exit backwards, which was accompanied by a mad rush at the door.

Many lion and tiger tamers were injured or worse. In 1850, Wombwell's seventeen-year-old niece, Ellen Bright, died in Chatham while trying to emulate her famous uncle. The inquest into her death took place at the regrettably named Golden Lion Inn and the jury heard how the tiger 'had seized her furiously by the neck, inserting the teeth of the upper jaw in her chin and closing his mouth, inflicting frightful injury in the throat by his fangs'.

In 1856, Wombwell's was sited in Broughton Park opposite Bellevue Terrace and a local resident wrote to *The Scotsman*:

> I live near Broughton Park, and so do the elephants, tigers, monkeys, &c., which compose Wombwell's Menagerie. I am not complaining. Night or day I am not disturbed by these newcomers. But being a universal philanthropist, I cannot help speaking out in behalf of my less fortunate neighbours whose equanimity may be disturbed by this strange colony. Just figure to yourself, Sir, an old lady retiring to rest after a day of exhausting

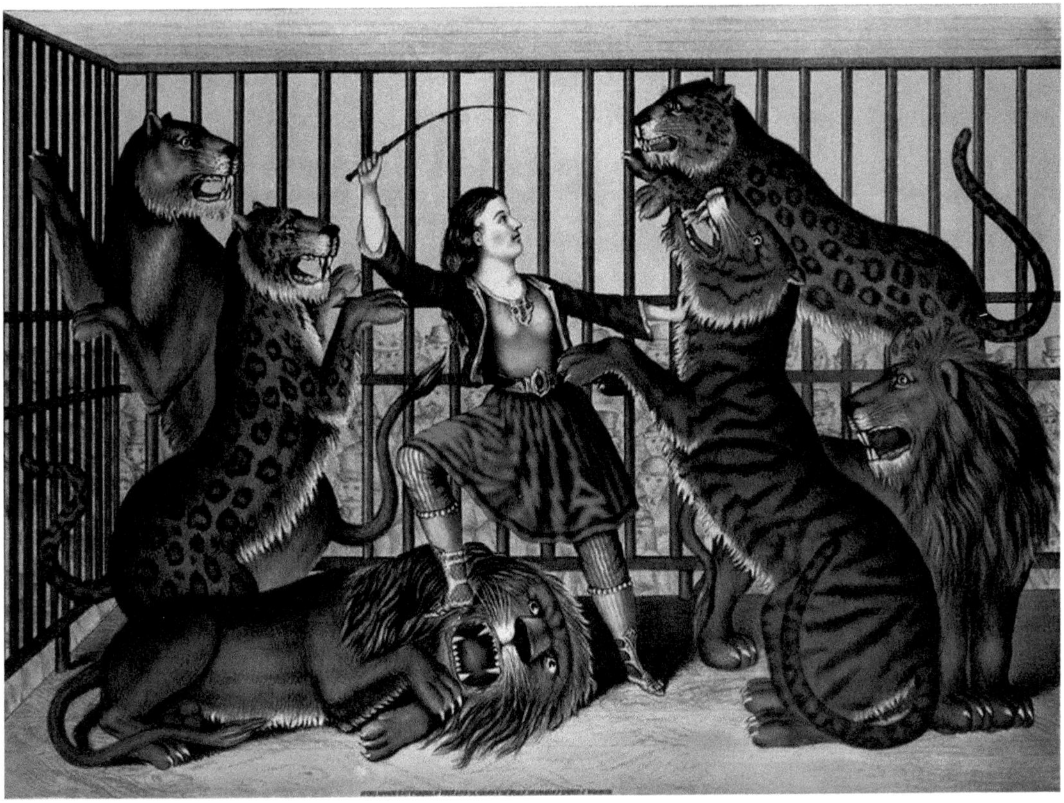

Ellen Bright, the Lion Queen.

> toil, or much more exhausting idleness ... the angry growl of a bear, or the supernatural squealing of innumerable wild cats suddenly and cruelly breaks her slumbers, communicating, at the same time, a disastrous shock to her nervous system! But the congregation of boys and women, attracted every evening to our neighbourhood, is an additional annoyance. Their yells and howls positively emulate those of their friends inside the curtains. Indeed, at times it is difficult to say from what class of individuals these noises proceed.

On 17 January 1863, James Turner, a printer, was hosting his annual dinner for his friends at Edinburgh's Café Royal. As everyone had eaten their fill the guests were surprised when towards the end of the evening a 'very large-sized pie, handsomely ornamented with a crimson cloth' was brought in. Their surprise turned to exclamations of astonishment when the waiter whipped off the pie's top to reveal five lion cubs nestling in the dish. The cubs had been born eight days earlier to a lioness at William Manders' Menagerie that was exhibiting in Nicolson Street. Turner announced that the lions were to be publicly christened before the assembled company. After they were named Robert Burns, Sir William Wallace, Sir Walter Scott, Princess Alexandra and Lord Clyde, 'a libation of port wine was poured over their noses'. The cuddly cubs then were 'handed round the company for inspection', before being 'carefully wrapped up in a warm cloth' and taken back to the menagerie in a cab.

After George Wombwell died his wife managed the menagerie until 1866 and then passed the business on to Alexander Fairgrieve, an Edinburgh man, whose wife, Harriet Bright, was Mrs Wombwell's niece, and the sister of Ellen who had been killed by the tiger in 1850. Fairgrieve sold the menagerie in 1872 and the animals were auctioned in Edinburgh's Waverley Market. Thomas Frost described the sale in his book, *The Old Showmen and the Old London Fairs:*

> A sale of wild beasts is an event so novel that it excited considerable attention, not only in Edinburgh, but all over the country. Buyers were numerous, and included well-known naturalists, circus proprietors, and representatives of zoos in Britain, America and France. Perhaps the most prominent was Mr Jamrach, the most extensive dealer in wild animals in the world ... The auctioneer commenced the sale with the monkeys, which were recommended as pets for the drawing-room, as lively, frisky and intelligent ... The oldest inhabitant in the establishment was the condor, who had been attached to Wombwell's Menagerie for forty years, and despite his age he fetched £15 ... Mr Jamrach secured the magnificent performing tigress 'Tippoo' for £155 ... The black-maned lion 'Hannibal', six and a half years old, said to be the finest and largest in Britain, was started at £50, and the bidding was comparatively slow for a time. On reaching £225,

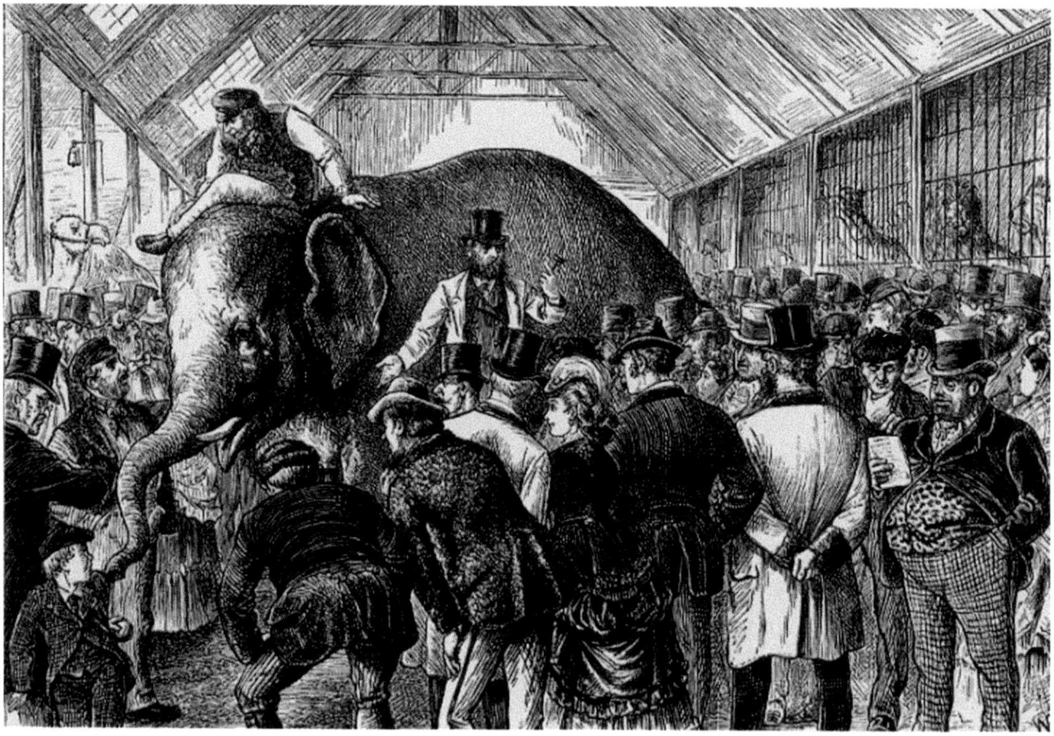

The Wombwell animal auction, 1872. (Courtesy of *Illustrated London News*)

> the auctioneer said he was ashamed of such a ridiculously small price being offered for the finest lion in the world, and he was sure that 'Hannibal' was as disgusted as he was, and would turn his back on the crowd. Sure enough, the animal did at that moment deliberately turn round, and the amusing episode created some liveliness in the bidding. 'Hannibal' was eventually knocked down for £270, to be sent to the Zoological Gardens in Bristol ... Competition for the large performing elephant, Maharajah, was limited, and this was the only animal which was sold much below its value. For a time the bidding rested at £380 till a suggestion was made that a prominent butcher should invest and introduce a new elephant sausage. The vision of mammoth sausages quickened the offers and by dint of perseverance, the figure reached £680, at which price Mr Jennison secured it for his Manchester zoo.

The total amount realised for the animals was £2,900 (£250,000 at today's value). All the animals then had to be dispatched to their various destinations and Maharajah, the elephant, was booked to travel to Manchester by train. But as Richard Bell recounts in his book *My Strange Pets* this did not go as planned:

> I saw the keeper start with it to send it off by train, a horse-box having been secured for this purpose. Some time elapsed, and the keeper appeared again in the menagerie, accompanied by the elephant. When asked why he had returned, he explained that no sooner was the huge beast put into the horse-box than he smashed the front part with his head, and the back end with his tail-end, and that the railway company refused to

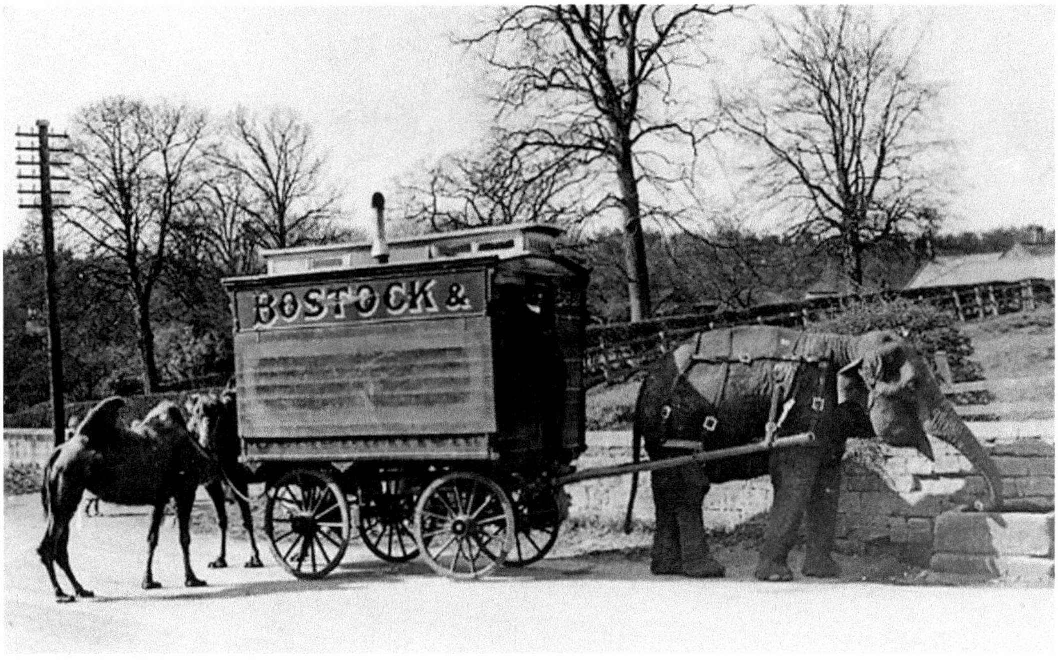

Bostock Menagerie caravan, *c.* 1910.

> have anything more to do with it. It was then resolved that the beast must go by road, and a discussion arose as to the best route. As I knew the country roads to England well, I suggested he should go by the old coach road between Scotland and England.

Jennison took Bell's advice and Maharajah, led by his handler, walked all the way south in ten days, cheered by large crowds.

When the last menagerie to visit Edinburgh came in 1914, *The Scotsman wrote*: 'It is like harking back to the old times, when a menagerie comes to town. The menagerie, in common with other institutions, has suffered the vicissitudes of time and change.'

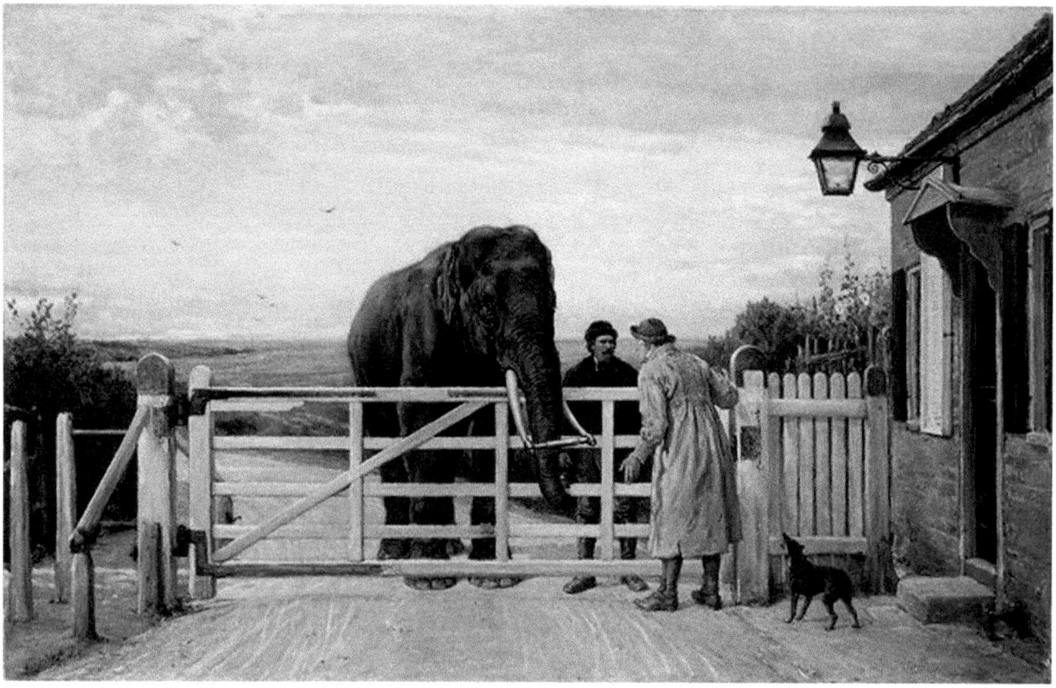

The Disputed Toll (Maharajah walking to Manchester) by Heywood Hardy. (Manchester Art Gallery)

4. Edinburgh's First Zoo and Aquarium

The word 'zoo' was first used by the London Zoological Gardens, which opened for scientific study in 1828, and the concept of permanent enclosures where a variety of wild animals could be viewed became fashionable. In 1838 a group formed with the aim of establishing a zoo in Edinburgh. The following year they gathered together a small and disparate collection of animals, including a Persian cat, a red deer, various monkeys, a buffalo and a golden eagle, and housed these in an unused wooden structure that had

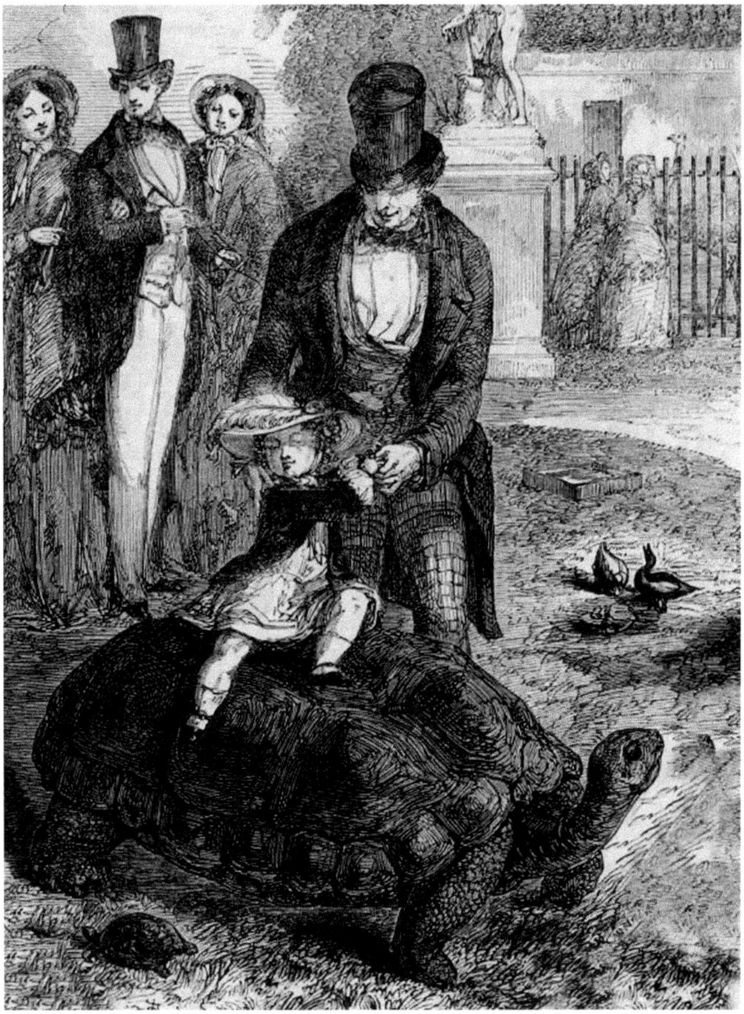

A child riding the land tortoise at the zoo.

been erected by an equestrian circus a few months before. In July 1839, the *Caledonian Mercury* reported on the situation:

> So interesting was the exhibition in a temporary building on the Earthen Mound that numbers, including many scientific individuals, daily flocked to witness it. The charge was judiciously limited to a trifling sum so that the working and all classes were enabled to gratify their laudable curiosity. It appears however, that the Board of Trustees for Encouraging the Arts and Manufactures who are proprietors of the Royal Institution Buildings in the vicinity had insisted on the removal of the wooden building in which the animals were temporarily accommodated. The consequence was that the valuable collection was somewhat suddenly ejected, in as far as no time was given to prepare other accommodation. Previous to this crisis the Directors had been fortunate to obtain an advantageous offer of the East Princes Street Garden from Messrs Cleghorn. No locality could be more favourable for the purposes of a Zoological Garden than the one selected, because it is not only in a central part of the town, and thus of easy access to citizens and strangers, but the grounds are spacious, airy and decorated with a fine plantation and shrubbery.

The proposed site was in the garden created in 1832 by Thomas Cleghorn, a seedsman, on open land to the east of the Earthen Mound. However, there was opposition and the newspaper's argument in favour of the idea has parallels in today's debates about proposed city innovations:

> Two or three respectable individuals still hesitate to lend their consent, and the operations of the Directors are thus necessarily retarded. We deeply regret that any difficulty should be thrown in the way of what may yet prove, as far as Scotland is concerned, a national institution; of its advantages to Edinburgh, even in the vulgar view of pecuniary interest, there can be little doubt. How many thousands have been expended in rearing monuments to the illustrious, and otherwise adorning the town; or, to come nearer to the present object, what solicitude is not evinced for the maintenance and extension of the University Museum, and the other depositories for all that is valuable, curious, and subservient to the advancement of science, literature, and art. Do not such as these institutions contribute to the attractions of the Modern Athens, drawing many, who have no especial tie to any other place, to pitch their residence here, and besides holding out an inducement to strangers to visit the capital.

In the end the opposition to the zoo being sited on Princes Street won the day, but the members of the newly constituted Edinburgh Zoological Gardens Association were determined and raised sufficient funds from subscribers to purchase 6 acres of land at Broughton Park on East Claremont Street. The project was overseen by Mr Atkins, who owned a large zoo in Liverpool, and his workmen landscaped the gardens and built structures to house the animals. Atkins enhanced the collection by bringing a number of animals from his zoo, including two lions, an elephant and a crocodile. The zoo was designed as a place where the great and the good of the city could promenade. When the zoo opened in July 1840, 'the roads

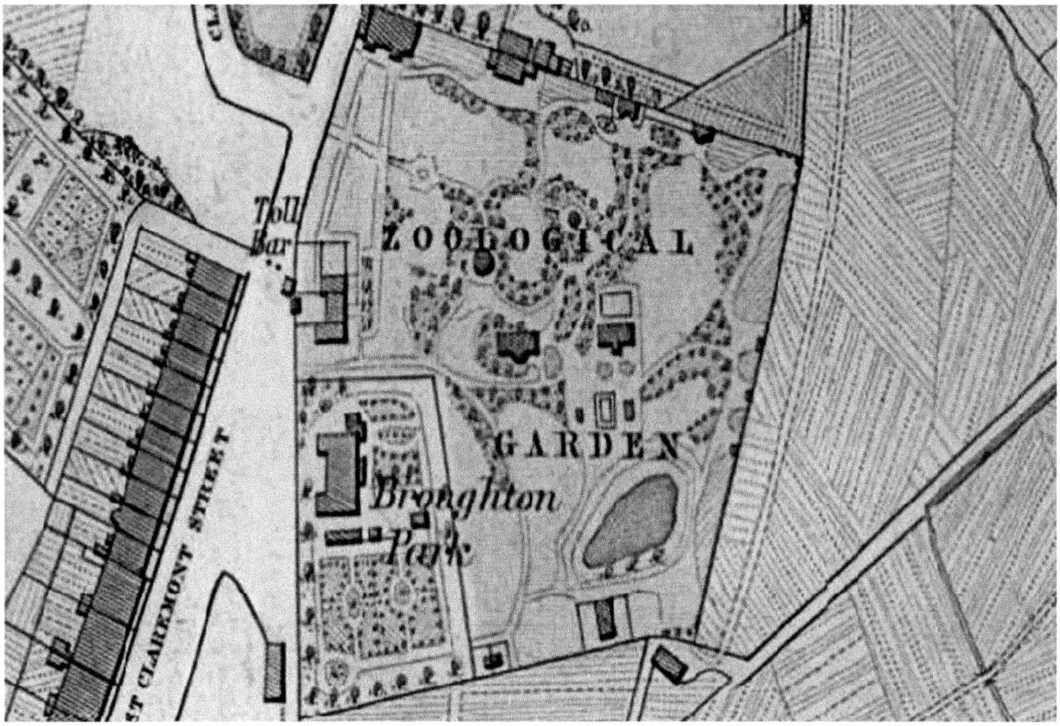

Map showing the zoo in 1850.

leading to the ground presented a continued current of elegantly dressed company, while the carriages stretched along the whole of Claremont Street'. Two army bands serenaded the visitors while the elephant 'quietly marched upon the green sward, supplying himself with nourishment, by mowing the grass with his proboscis'. In its first months the zoo included a large working model of Mount Vesuvius that recreated the 'eventful stages of the eruption, finishing with a terrific rush of molten lava down the mountain!'

The zoo's animal collection expanded through donations. In 1841, a tigress from Bengal was sent by Lieutenant-Colonel Borthwick of the Madras Army and its arrival was written up in the city's newspapers: 'To give an idea of the ravages which this formidable tenant of the jungle must make on other animals in catering for its subsistence, it may be stated that, during the voyage of 116 days, it consumed thirty-one sheep, twelve dozen fowls, three pigs, and eight cwt. of fish.'

One evening John Bowser, a joiner employed at the zoo, visited the tiger. Being a little inebriated he decided to stroke the tiger's face as a friendly gesture. Unfortunately, the tiger was not feeling as friendly and seized Bowser's hand with his teeth and then began to chew his way up the screaming man's arm. Zoo staff rushed to the scene and eventually managed to prise the tiger's jaws apart. John was rushed to the infirmary where his lower arm had to be amputated.

Further animals arrived. Lord Lurgan presented the zoo with a pair of Egyptian geese; Sir Alexander Duff gave three fallow deer; a land tortoise came from Mr Ball of Falkirk;

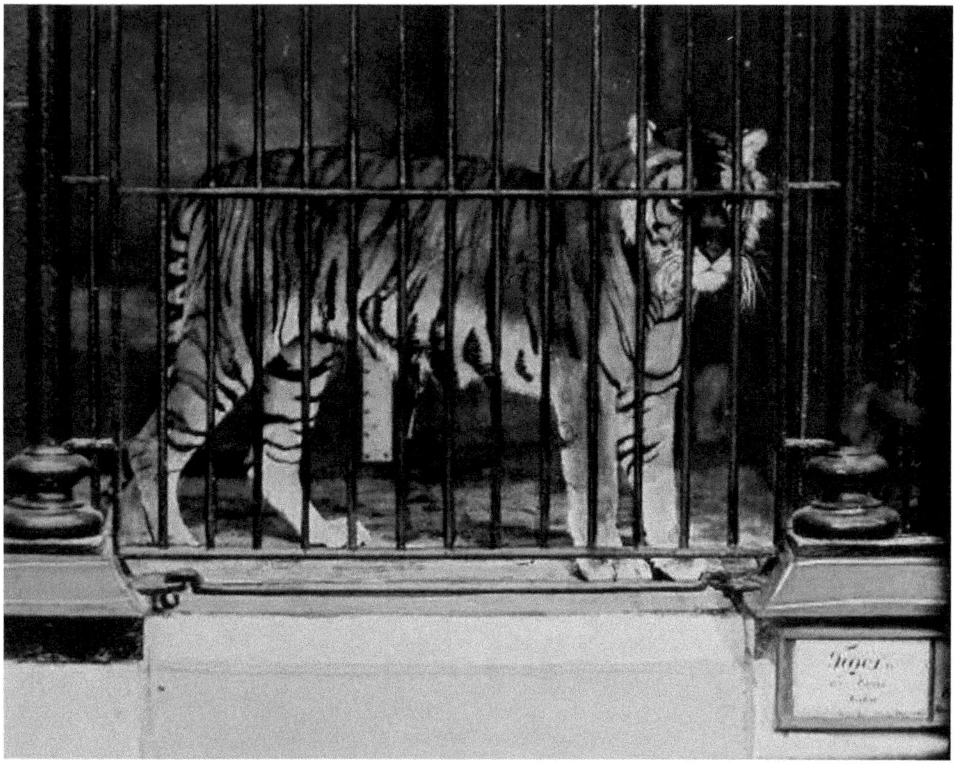

Bengal tiger in the zoo, *c.* 1870.

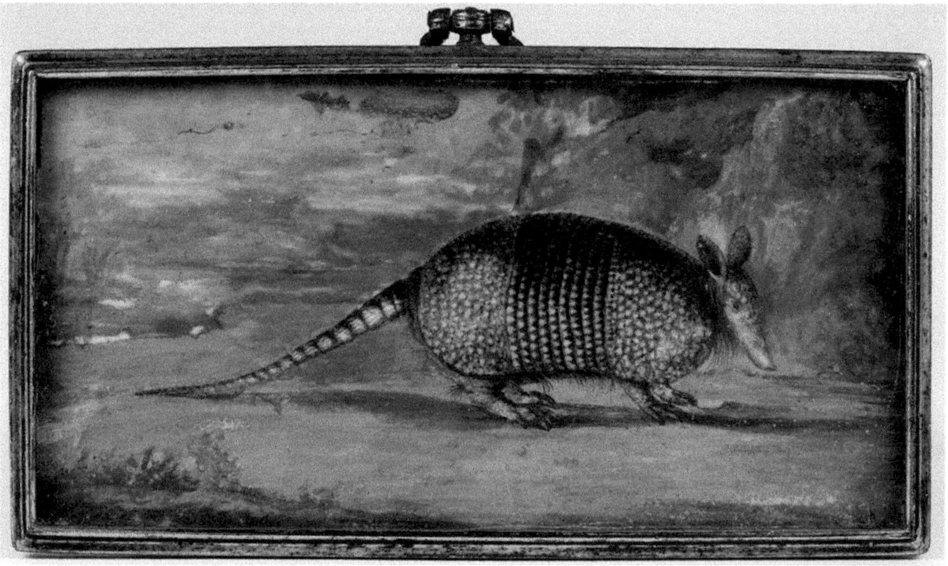

Miniature watercolour on ivory depicting an armadillo, 1763, inscribed, 'This creature, called the American armadillo, was brought from the Mosquito Shore to Lord Southwell, who presented it to the Prince of Wales.

and Miss Dalyell donated six parrots. The zoo had some success in breeding, including the births of three leopard cubs and two polar bear cubs. The zoo also purchased animals, including 'the singular and curious animal, the armadillo; it is an excessively active creature and being perfectly gentle and inoffensive, is occasionally indulged with a run through the gardens'. However, the finances were problematic and in 1852 a public meeting was held to explore the zoo's future at which the chairman explained that the initial borrowing to establish the zoo was still owed. Nothing was resolved and the zoo continued in spite of the financial concerns.

By 1858 the display included two tigers, a lioness, a leopard, two bears, a racoon, two emus and various other animals and birds. However, neither these nor the musical performances by army bands were sufficient incentive to attract the number of visitors required. To try to survive, the zoo began hiring the gardens out for exhibitions and mounted special attractions. In 1858, a representation of the siege, storming and capture of Delhi took place:

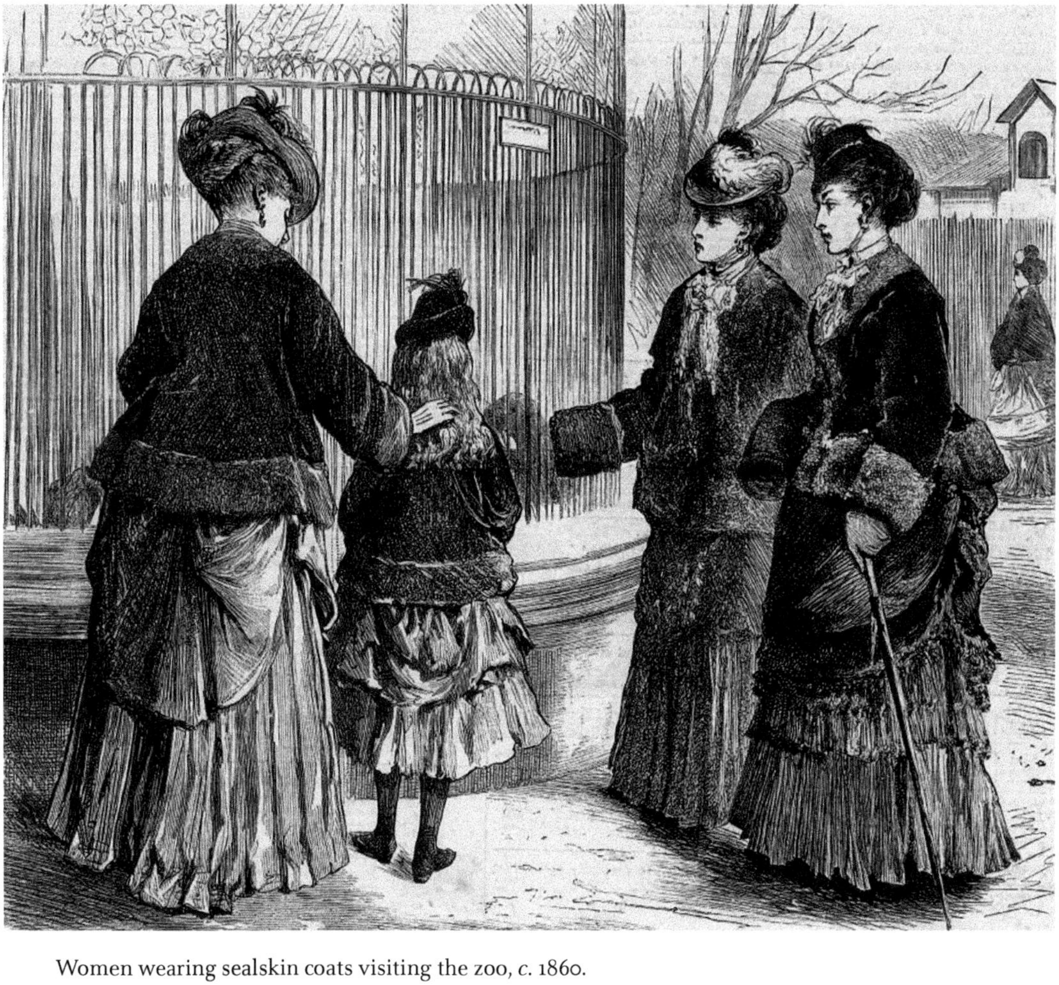

Women wearing sealskin coats visiting the zoo, *c.* 1860.

> A representation of the city was erected with fictitious walls … Bombshells were fired at each side; the British soldiers poured their shot against the city walls and the artillery sent forth its terrific sound. The Cashmere Gate was blown up and the victorious British troops rushed in. The effect was most magnificent and the display gave a pretty correct idea, on a very small scale of course, of what the famous siege actually was like.

The pyrotechnics at such events as this, plus many regular firework displays, must have been distressing for the animals and also the conditions in which the animals were being kept deteriorated.

By 1860 a London journal reported that the zoo was 'a disgrace both to the Zoological Science and to the humanity of Edinburgh'. The decline was due to the zoo's poor financial position and eventually the tigers and a number of the other larger animals were sold to Edmond's Menagerie. *The Scotsman* wrote: 'The glory of the gardens has departed. Monkeys, bear, and other specimens of the animal kingdom, have gradually been brought under the hammer, or sunk under the accumulated griefs of their fallen state, and save a few woebegone rabbits with dirty fur, and two or three Cochin China fowls, whose gauntness is almost spectral, nothing else remains to remind of its of better days.' The zoo closed in 1861.

Apart from ichthyologists (those who study fish), for most people before 1850 fish meant food or sport. However, an exhibition of ornate aquaria in cast-iron frames as part of the Great Exhibition of 1851 stimulated a wide interest in growing aquatic plants and keeping fish. 'Every drawing room has its aquarium, and young ladies talk learnedly of radiaria and zoophyta, and of their charmingly bright acaliphae.'

In the 1870s a fashion for large aquariums arose, and from Brighton to Rothesay investors rushed to support these new attractions. In 1875, the Edinburgh Theatre, Winter Garden and Aquarium raised funding to build the first phase of the project – a theatre seating 2,300 people in Castle Terrace – but the aquarium was never built. A couple of years later a Mr Brechin approached the city council to build an aquarium in an unused part of the recently opened Waverley Vegetable Market. It opened in 1878. 'The visitor enters into a space that has the effect of producing a delightful combination of grotto, aquarium and fernery. Constructed of tufa stone it presents the appearance of a stalactite cavern.' It had a seal tank 40 by 80 feet and sixteen smaller tanks that held tench, carp, pike, trout, turtles, seahorses, crustaceans, newts and a shoal of herring. Not long after opening there was great excitement when a tope shark gave birth to four baby sharks.

As had been the case with the zoo, the marine exhibits do not seem to have been sufficient to draw the required number of visitors. In 1882, part of the seal tank was converted into 'a bijou theatre' that housed performances by magicians, puppets and trained pigeons. Even such attractions as Professor Johnson and the Lady Swimmers performing in the seal tank could not save the aquarium and it closed in 1884. The seal tanks were brought back into action in 1898 for performances by Captain Woodward's Sea Lions: 'A truly marvellous performance. See the unique seal orchestra. See them juggle, smoke, sing, and perform many other marvellous feats'. *The Edinburgh Evening News* visited:

> Wandering behind the stage the next thing to attract the attention were Captain Woodward's performing sea lions. Three were in a corner going through a practice

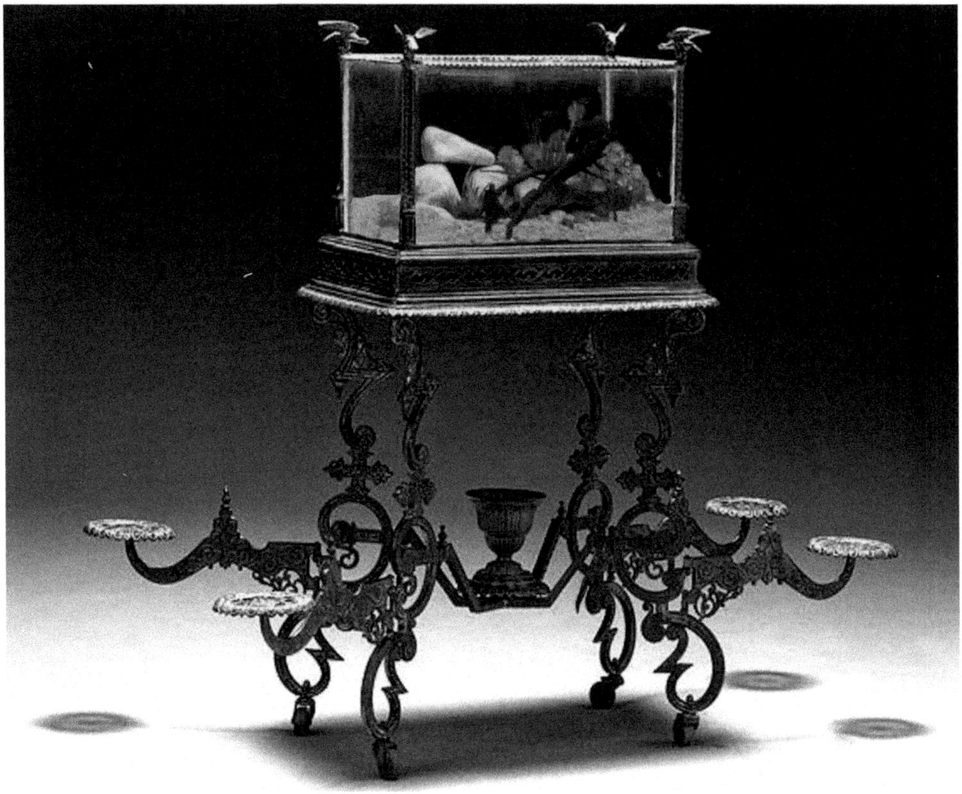

Victorian cast-iron aquarium, *c.* 1870.

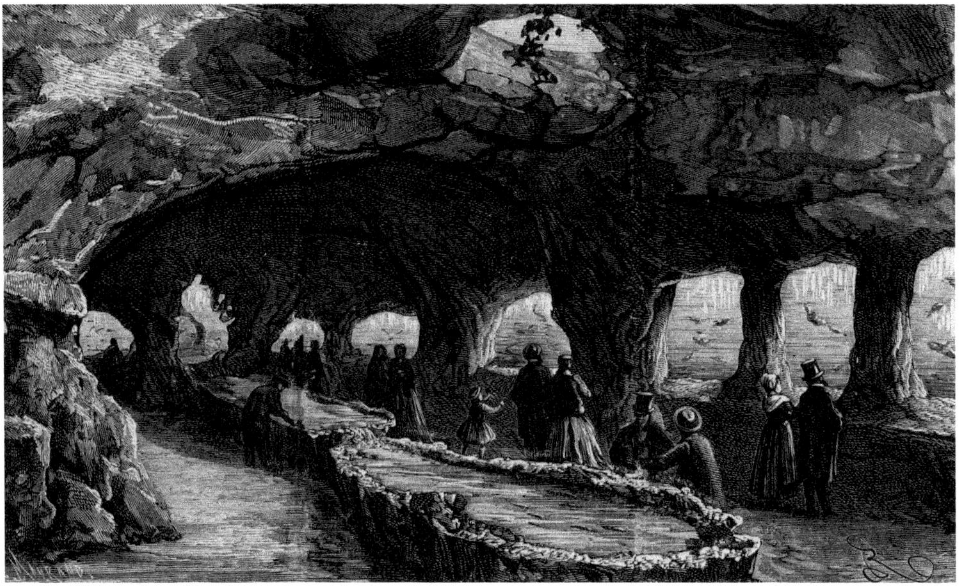

Aquarium interior, *c.* 1870.

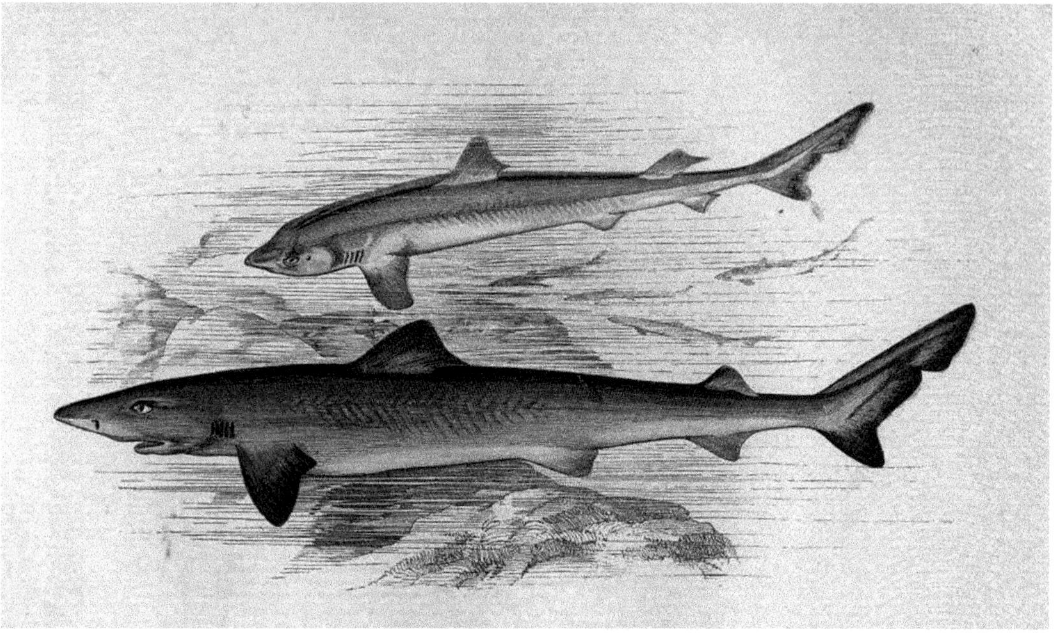

Tope shark engraving by Jonathan Couch, 1862.

> performance and another three were confined in the wire-covered tank. The imprisoned ones were uttering short dog-like barks, apparently in approval of their comrades' efforts, while beside the ones outside stood the Captain. He was quite ready to speak on the subject of his pets, for he believes in making them perform through kindness and not abuse. The sea lions have been in captivity for about five years, but they seem to like it, though the changes in climate they have to encounter when travelling about is not good for them. 'And what about learning tricks; do they take to these quickly?' I asked. 'They are,' he replied, 'very shy and retiring creatures, and take some time before they can summon enough courage to face an audience. Some learn the tricks in a short period; others again take longer. This fellow here,' he added, as he patted the head of large glossy-coated animal, 'does the ball-trick, and it took him about a year to learn. They are very inquisitive, and despite all our attempts to hide the food from them, it is soon discovered, and unless at once locked up, will soon disappear'.

In 1916, Captain Woodward approached the Royal Navy's Board of Invention and Research with a proposal that his animals could be trained to spot German U-boats. Woodward's recommendation was taken seriously, and experiments and trials took place in public swimming baths. The idea was to train the sea lions to link the sound of a submarine with food and swim towards it. However, the idea proved futile and was discontinued, although Woodward later advertised his performers as 'The Actual Admiralty U-boat Hunting Sea-Lions'.

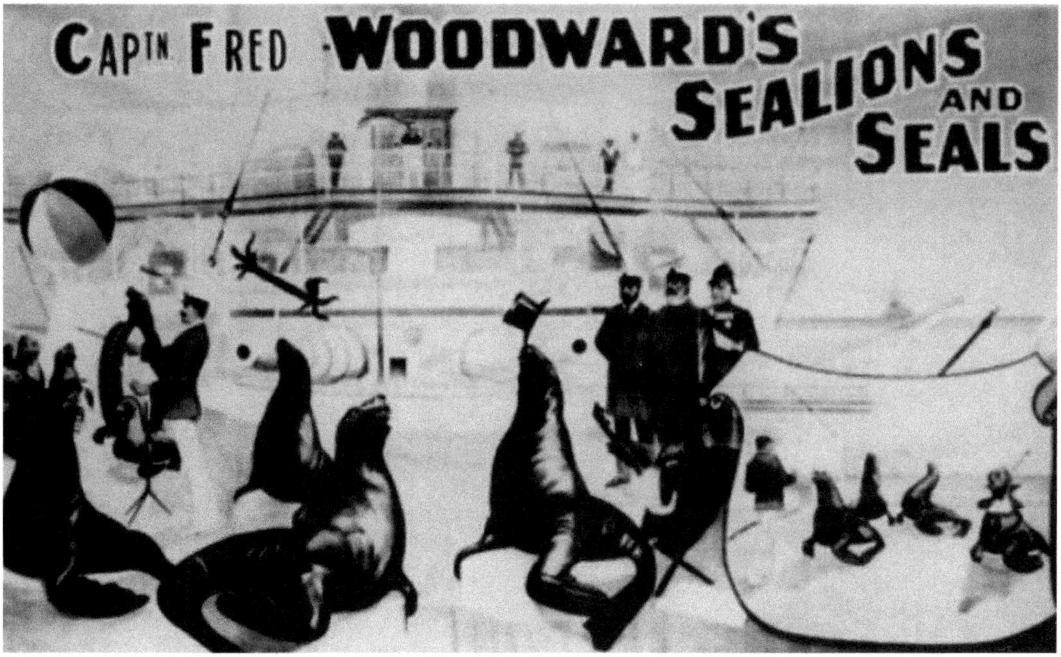

Poster for Woodward's sea lions and seals, *c.* 1900.

5. Edinburgh Zoo

It was the chance fall of a baby starling that brought into being Edinburgh Zoo at Corstorphine. The fledgling was cared for by a young boy, Thomas Hining Gillespie, and so began his lifelong interest in animals. Alongside his work as a solicitor Gillespie collected a variety of mammals and birds, and, unable to afford his own menagerie, began to explore the idea of a zoo. 'Some said that a Zoo would never do in the Edinburgh climate, but I knew that there had been a previous attempt,' Gillespie later recounted. Along with others enthused by the idea he established the Zoological Society of Edinburgh in 1909 and the society searched for a site. Corstorphine Hill House and its 80-acre estate on the east side of the hill became available but it was priced at £17,000 and the society had only managed to raise £6,000. Fortunately, as Edinburgh Council had discussed creating a zoo in one of the city parks ten years earlier but not taken the idea forward, the city agreed to buy the land and lease it to the society.

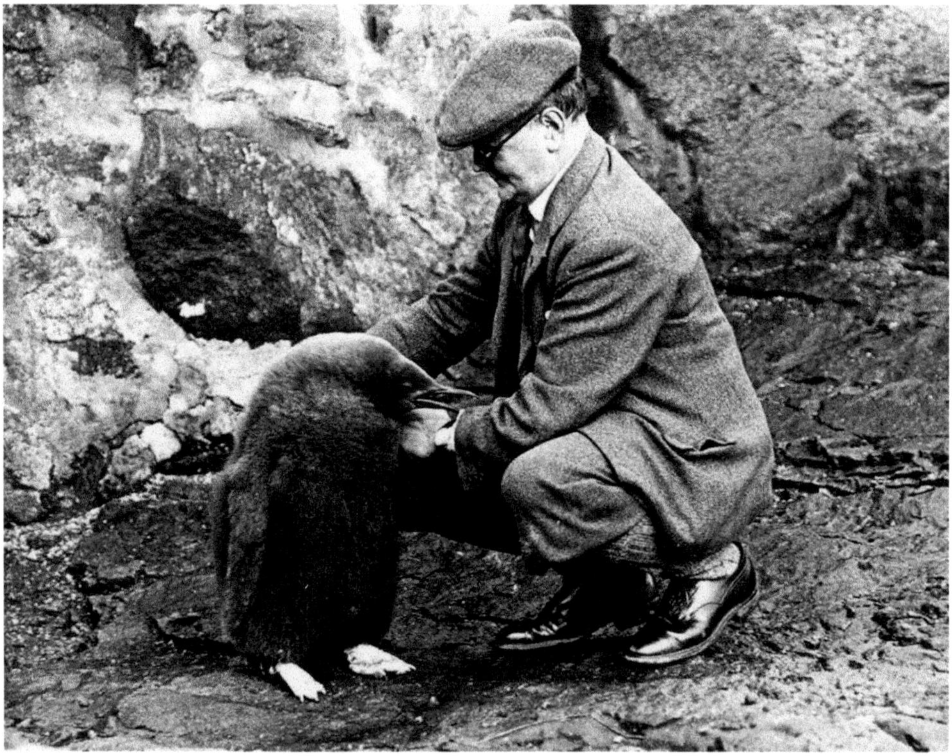

Thomas Hining Gillespie with the first king penguin chick, 1916. (Courtesy of Edinburgh Zoo)

The design of the zoo was influenced by the ideas of Carl Hagenbeck, a German who six years earlier had created near Hamburg what is now regarded as the first modern zoo. Hagenbeck's innovation was to create animal enclosures without bars and modelled as closely as possible to animals' natural habitats. The Corstorphine site was quarried to provide materials for the zoo's roads and the pits formed into enclosures for bears,

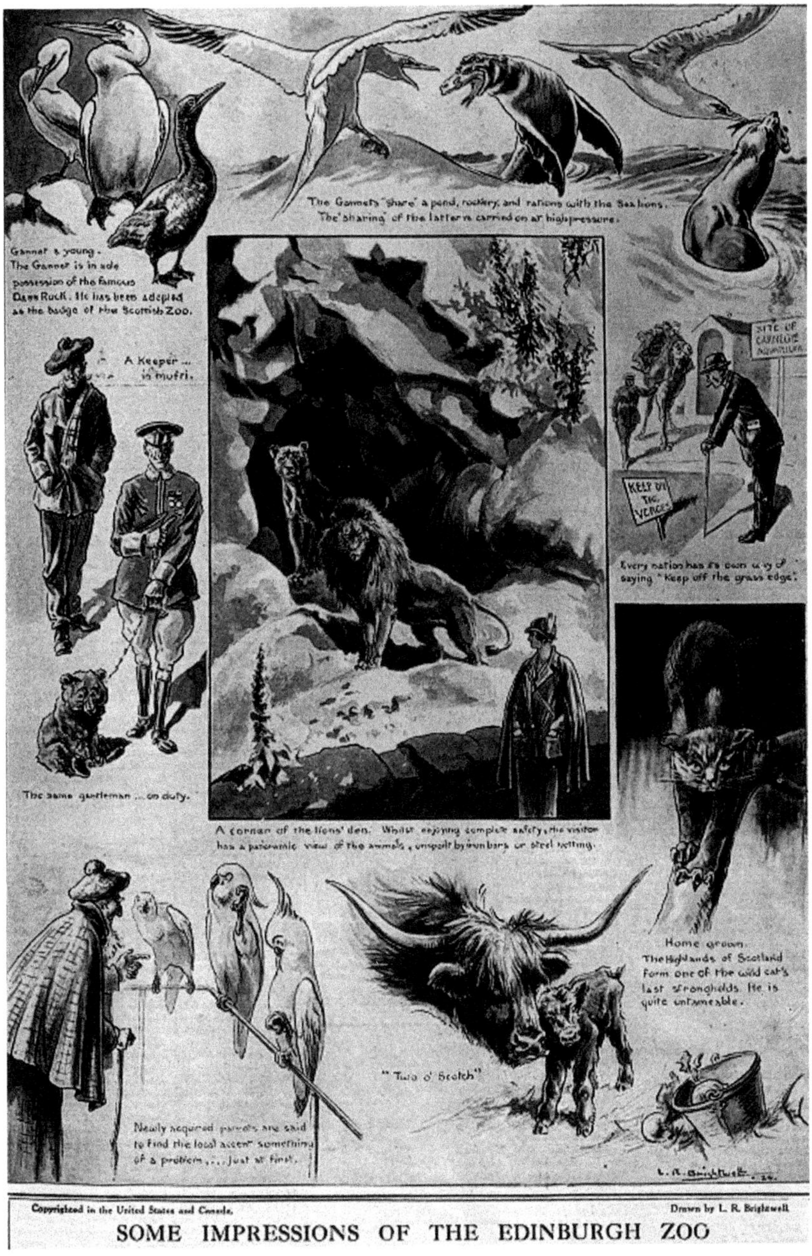

Impressions of Edinburgh Zoo on the cover of *The Graphic*, September 1924.

sea lions, polar bears, lions and others. In 1913, the zoo prepared to open to the public. Given that Scotland is home to around 60 per cent of Europe's gannets, it is appropriate that the first animal to be acquired was a gannet that cost 8*d*. More exotic creatures were bought and six lions, four bears, two hyenas, eight wolves, four leopards and other animals were borrowed from a private menagerie owner in Kent. Gillespie described their arrival: 'The lions' cages had no doors fixed and men had sat on the animals' travelling boxes holding the doors until gates were brought and fixed.' Later, after all the animals had been housed in their enclosures, a wolf was found wandering round the grounds as the workmen had forgotten to concrete the floors, allowing the wolf to burrow out. A number of farm animals were shown, including a black Shetland ewe that had the honour of being the first to give birth in the zoo.

Visitors were amazed to see a retriever dog in the cage with the lions and some complained. However, the practice was common at the time as lionesses and tigresses could only look after two to three cubs, and any extra were housed with a dog for company and often the dog stayed with the animal. One visitor noted the bond between the animals:

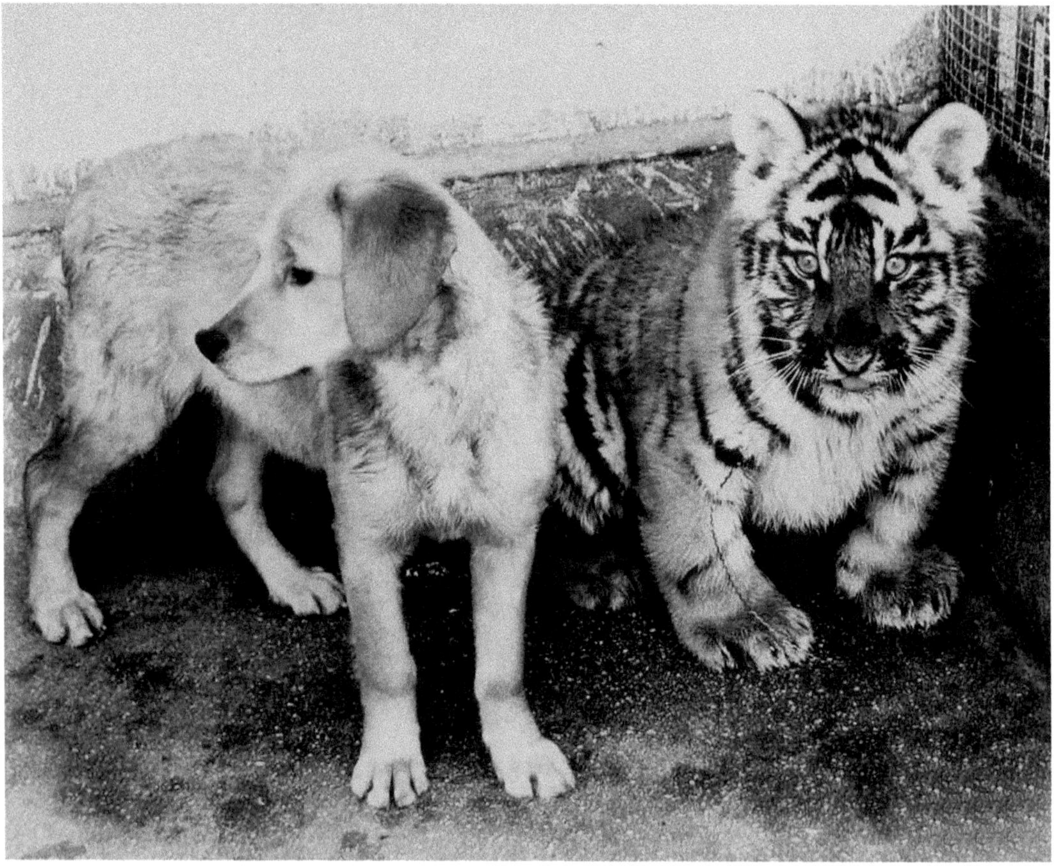

Dog and tiger cub share a cage.

> The dog was disporting itself most playfully with the larger of the two lions. The dog seemed to treat its fierce brother in the same way as it would playfully play with its master's hand in its mouth. Evidence of their brotherly love was proven as when the dog was removed the lion showed considerable resentment. In short, it was immediately transformed from a playful kitten into a roaring lion.

The Scottish diaspora was a significant factor in the zoo obtaining new animals. Soon after opening William Burn Murdoch, an Edinburgh-born artist, travel writer and explorer, brought the zoo a second polar bear. Murdoch participated in a number of Arctic and Antarctic expeditions and drew many humorous cartoons featuring polar bears. He was a keen musician and claimed to be the first person to have played the bagpipes in the

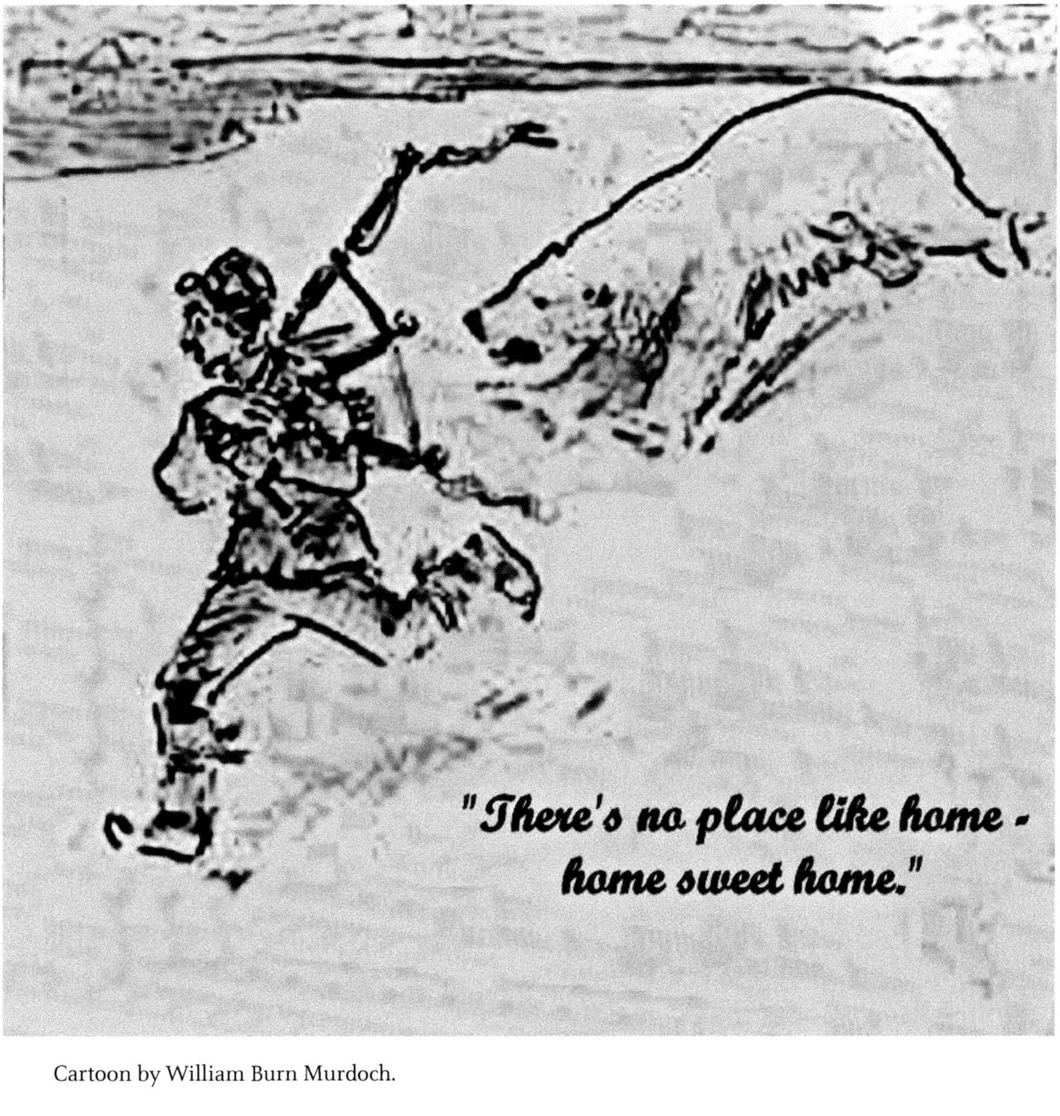

Cartoon by William Burn Murdoch.

Antarctic. One of those involved in establishing the zoo was Lord Salvensen, a Scottish lawyer, politician and judge who was instrumental in the zoo having the world's largest collection of penguins. His family owned a large whaling company and in 1914 one of the company's ships brought to Edinburgh four king penguins, a rockhopper, a gentoo and four elephant seals. Given the popularity of Edinburgh Zoo's penguins today *The Scotsman*'s article about their arrival was spot on:

> These strange and infrequently exhibited creatures promise to prove worthy rivals of the inmates of the monkey-house in providing amusement for onlookers. Nothing the members of the monkey tribe can do will be more amusing than the curious waddle of the young king penguins or the manner in which the older ones keep their ungainly figures motionless for long periods with their long bills pointing proudly skywards.

In 1919, one of the king penguins laid an egg that successfully hatched. This was the first captive breeding of this species anywhere in the world and it is for this reason that a king penguin is included in the zoo's logo. There were occasional escapes. In 1920, two sea lions slipped out of their enclosure and made a remarkable journey before being recaptured. Though they had no knowledge of the terrain the two descended the hill, exited the zoo, crossed the main Edinburgh to Glasgow road, wended their way past residential houses and found their way to the Water of Leith. This they achieved overnight, being spotted the next morning by a surprised local dog walker. Gillespie, who became the zoo's first director, said, 'I cannot conceive how they got to Roseburn Bridge, which is over a mile and a half away, in 11 hours.'

During the 1930s the zoo began to build up its collection of chimpanzees and was not averse to promoting them as entertainment for publicity purposes. In 1932, one chimpanzee, Bobo, was taken to Scottish Broadcasting House in Queen Street for the recording of the children's radio show *Radio Playtime*. Alongside a Punch and Judy show Bobo appeared on the stage wearing a tartan kilt and was vociferously applauded by the audience of children, although his act consisted simply of 'nibbling a sweet and drinking from a bottle of lemonade'. The zoo also introduced a 'Chimpanzee's Tea Party' as a visitor attraction. The idea had originated at London Zoo in 1927 and Edinburgh noted that its event was attracting 300 people, each paying sixpence. The zoo management thought that even just charging 3*d* would still bring a good profit.

One Saturday in 1934, Miss Wendy Wood walked into the zoo, smeared her face and hands with cod liver oil, wrapped a sealskin around herself and then emitted a strange cry. Given that Miss Wood was an advocate for Scottish Nationalism and earlier that year had burned a copy of the Treaty of Union between Scotland and England in Edinburgh's Parliament Square, one might presume this to be another political art event. However, the audience for Wood's apparently bizarre behaviour was a baby seal that had been caught by fishermen at St Abbs and taken to the zoo. The young seal had refused to be fed and Wood, who had learned to imitate a seal's cry while living in the Hebrides, believed she could trick it into taking milk from a bottle. At first the seal furiously attacked Miss Wood but by gentle coaxing and perseverance she eventually persuaded the seal to drink and saved its life.

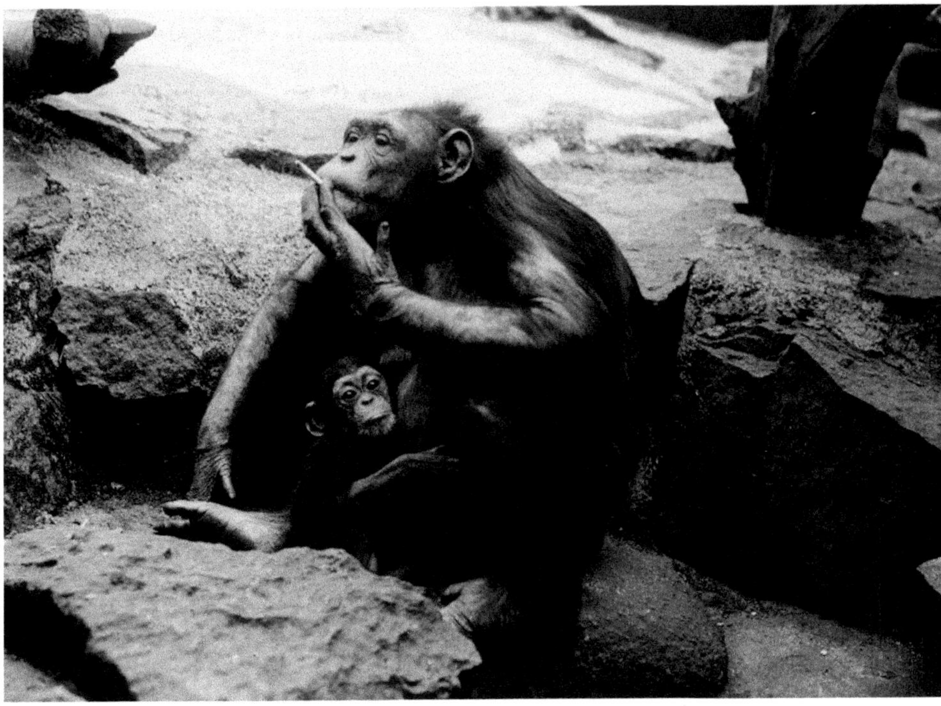

Above: Wednesday the chimpanzee smoking. (Courtesy of Edinburgh Zoo)

Right: Guinness Edinburgh Zoo poster by John Gilroy, 1950.

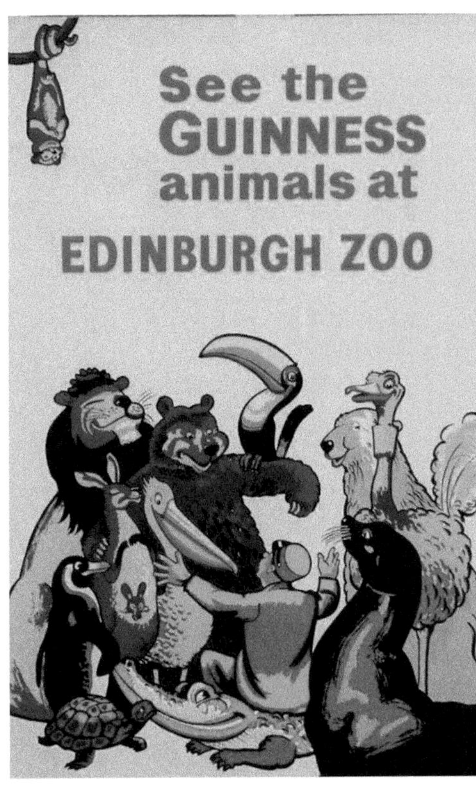

Edinburgh Zoo welcomed its first giraffe in 1938. He was named George and, being the only giraffe in the zoo, a collection box was set up next to his cage seeking donations to buy him a wife. Sadly, in spite of many pennies from children, George died in 1941 before he had saved enough to marry. At the outbreak of the Second World War concern about dangerous animals escaping from the zoo due to bomb damage led to the poisonous snakes and wolves being destroyed. Armed guards patrolled ready to shoot any other dangerous animals in the event of escape. Two bombs did fall on the zoo late in 1940 and it was rumoured that two lions, an elephant and George the giraffe had been killed, but the casualty list was, in reality, six budgies and a wild rabbit.

More of a concern for the zoo was wartime food rationing. While ration coupons for feed for horses, mules, donkeys and asses were issued, pet owners had to use part of their allowance to feed their animals, as did the zoo. Several of the zoo's animals were 'adopted' by schoolchildren and others, and they used some of their coupons to buy appropriate food for their chosen animal. The 1923 song 'Yes! We Have No Bananas' became popular

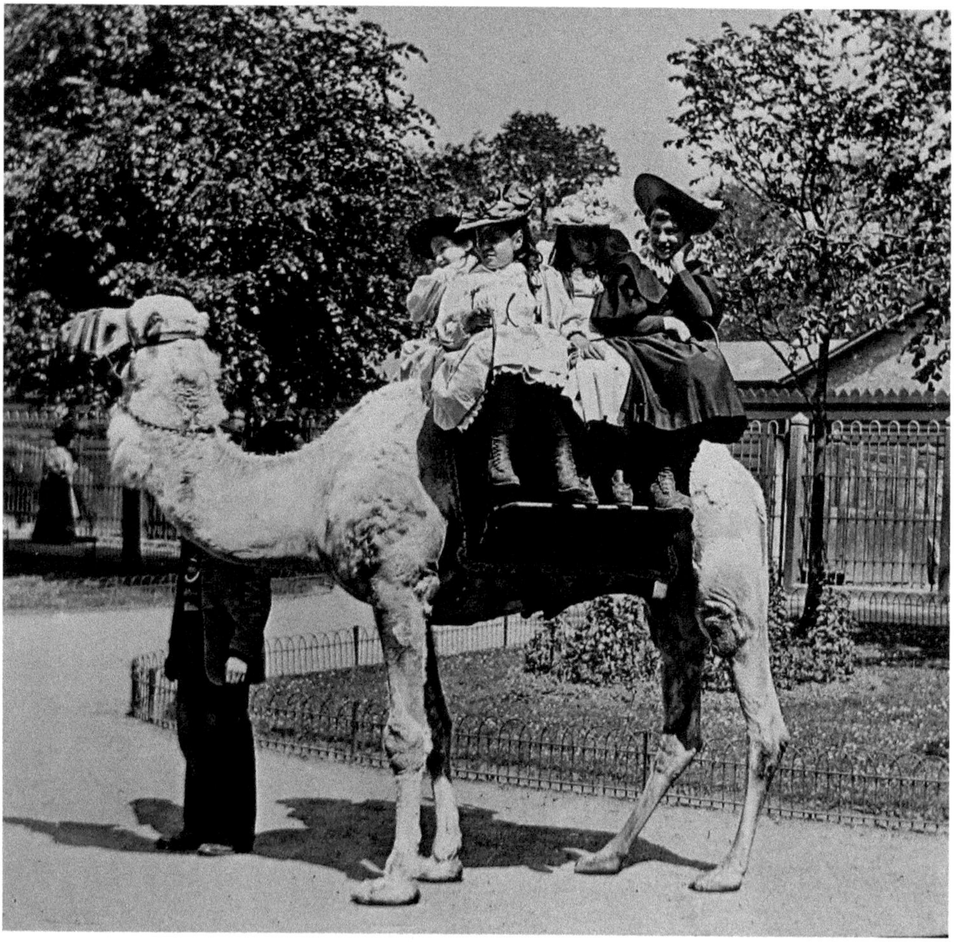

Camel ride at the zoo, *c.* 1900. (Photo A. Baird)

in Britain following a complete ban on the import of the fruit in November 1940 as the refrigerated ships that normally transported fruit were needed for the war effort. This was a calamity for many of the animals at the zoo as in 1938 they had consumed 162,720 bananas and 14,000 oranges, but during the war had to go without.

The zoo's famous Penguin Parade came about by chance in 1951. The keeper accidently left the gate to the penguins' enclosure open and one of the gentoos decided to investigate the rest of the zoo, and when he waddled out the other penguins followed. Amused, the keeper decided to see where they went and all who saw the procession were so entertained, it became a regular event. In 1961, the Norwegian's King's Guard visited the Edinburgh Tattoo and a lieutenant, Nils Egelien, became interested in the zoo's penguin colony. When the guards returned to Edinburgh in 1972 Egelien arranged for one of the penguins to be adopted as a mascot by the regiment and it was named Nils Olav in honour of Egelien and Olav V of Norway. Nils Olav has been promoted each time the King's Guard has returned to Edinburgh. Following the death of the original penguin it was agreed that the tradition should continue, and the second Nils Olav reached the rank

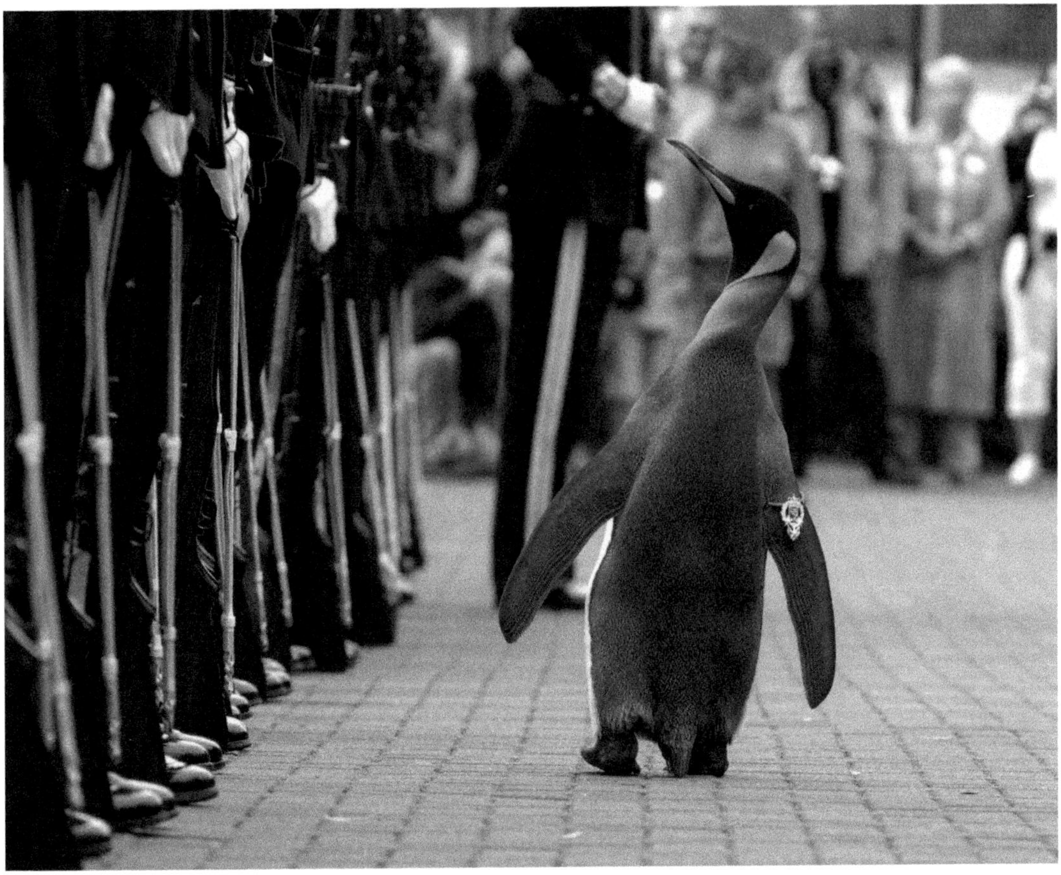

Sir Nils Olav inspecting the King's Guard of Norway in 2008. (Courtesy of Majoritems under Open Government Licence 1.0)

of colonel-in-chief. In 2008, Harald V approved a knighthood and Sir Nils Olav II became the first penguin to receive such an honour. A bronze statue of the first Nils Olav sits outside Penguins' Rock.

The arrival of two Giant Pandas in 2011 was regarded as a coup both for the zoo and the Scottish government, although not all were impressed. The pandas initially were housed below the rock-hopper penguins' enclosure and the penguins, perhaps jealous of no longer being the main attraction, began directing their droppings on to the people queuing to view the new arrivals.

Today television provides magnificent documentaries showing animals in the wild and in 1998 a two-month study at the zoo explored how the chimpanzees responded to such documentaries. Each day a group were shown one of six fifteen-minute videos, all consisting of extracts from David Attenborough documentaries about chimpanzees. Within a week the four females eagerly settled down to watch the videos while the males continued their normal activities. However, after six weeks, even the female tele-addicts became bored with the repeats.

Some argue that all zoos should be closed but Sir David Attenborough has disagreed, stressing that seeing animals in documentaries cannot compare to seeing the real thing. 'Only the sight of a creature in the flesh can give us a true understanding of its nature', he said. Throughout its hundred plus years Edinburgh Zoo has given visitors that opportunity. As more and more species are threatened with extinction in their natural environment, zoos act as valuable wildlife conservation agencies, providing safe havens and breeding programmes to help sustain species at risk.

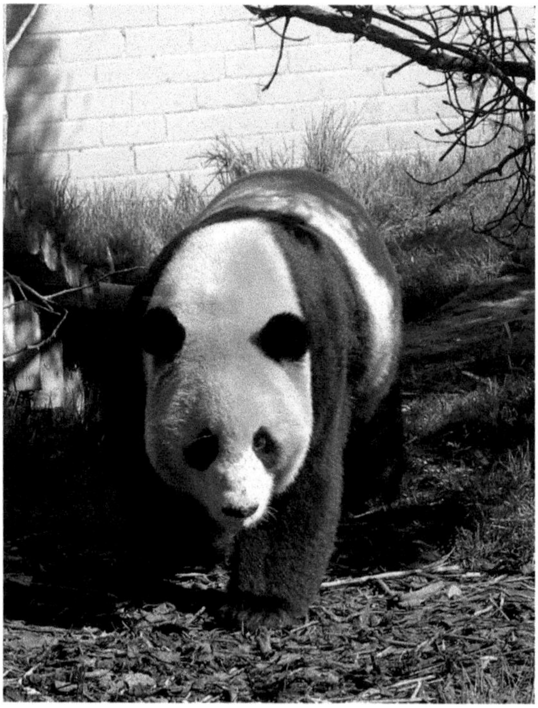

Panda at Edinburgh Zoo, 2014.

6. Performing Animals

In Edinburgh in 1596 Patrick Henderson recorded: 'There came an Englishman to Edinburgh, with a chestain-coloured naig, which he called Marocco. He made him to do many rare and uncouth tricks, such as never horse was observed to do the like before in this land.' This was William Banks's famous horse named Marocco that he had trained to do a number of tricks including walking on two legs: distinguishing between colours: counting coins and indicating numbers on thrown dice; and at the end of the act baring its teeth, whinnying and chasing Banks offstage. In London his 'Thinking Horse' made Banks wealthy and famous.

In 1705, Adam Kerr, a baker and a burgess of Edinburgh, wrote a letter of complaint to the Edinburgh Dean of Guild Court about his neighbour's housing of an elephant above him in a tenement in Fishmarket Close. The animal's owner was a Dutchman, Abraham Sever, who, Kerr complained, 'keeps his elephant therein and exposes it. His Dung and water thereof comes so doun in great quantities upon the vault and spoyle and abuses the concerned goods'. The elephant had toured around Europe and when Sever arrived in Edinburgh he sought permission from the town council 'to expose

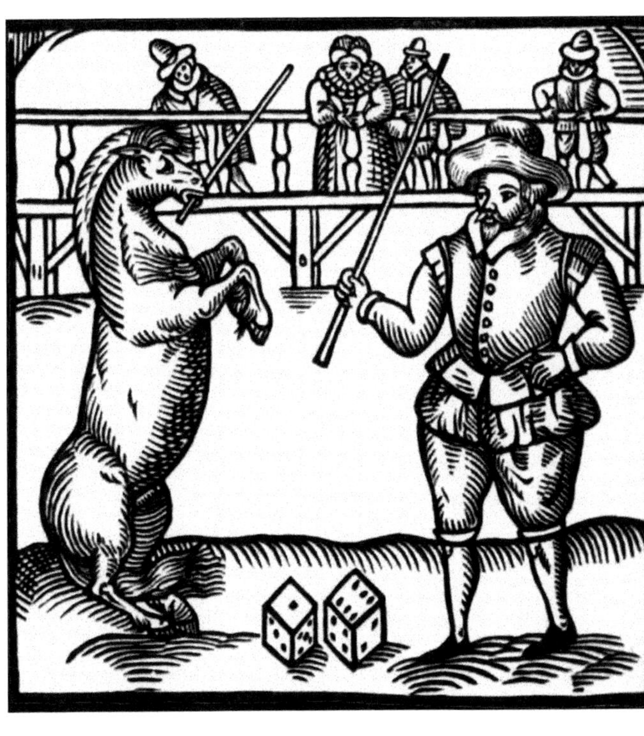

William Banks and Marocco.

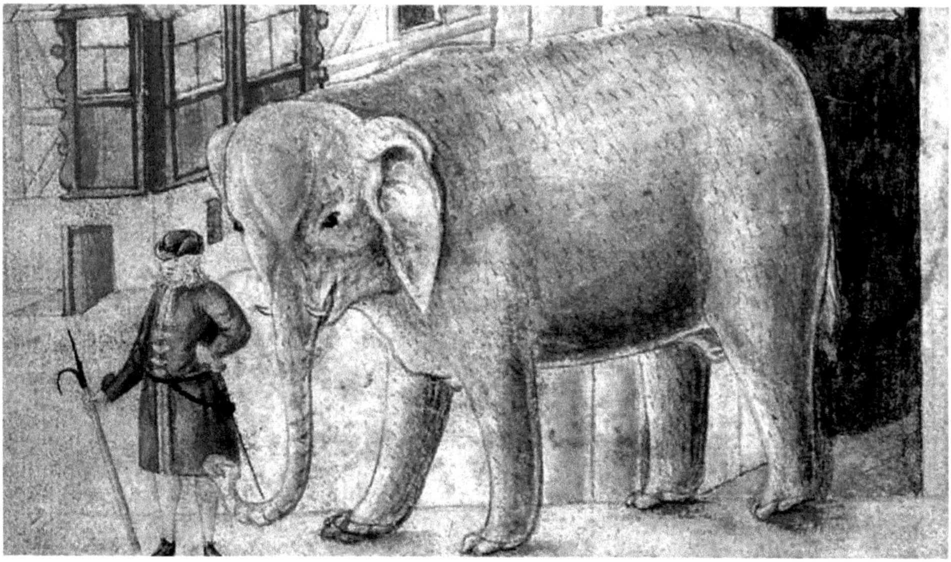

Abraham Sever and his elephant, by unknown artist.

his elephant to all persones within the toun and suburbs upon his payment of ane gratification to the kirk treasurer for the use of the poor'. The elephant had been trained to perform a variety of tricks:

> This wonderful Creature performs several Actions as swift & nimble as his Master commands him. First he takes his Masters Hat, Salutes the Company and makes Reverence upon his Knees ... He takes a piece of Money from the Ground and delivers it to his master. He kneels down to receive people upon his body, and bears two on his trunk, and two on his ears, and ten on his back.

Whether because of the baker's complaint or simply to find new paying spectators, Sever and the elephant left Edinburgh for Aberdeen. Perhaps due to the cold weather or the elephant's advanced age, the elephant died outside Dundee. A surgeon, Dr Patrick Blair, hearing of the animal's demise, arranged to undertake the first dissection of an elephant in Britain.

Over time the showing of performing animals moved indoors as it was easier to obtain payment from spectators, although some animals, usually monkeys and bears, were often exhibited in the street, usually by foreign itinerants. Most were made to perform a mockery of a dance and were notoriously badly treated by their owners.

In 1787, 'The Learned Pig' was exhibited in Edinburgh. The act was created in 1780 by a Scotsman, Samuel Bisset, who ran a travelling novelty show, and was an instant success:

> This entertaining and sagacious animal casts accounts by means of typographical cards, in the same manner as a printer composes, and by the same method sets down any capital or surname, reckons the number of people present, tells by evoking on a

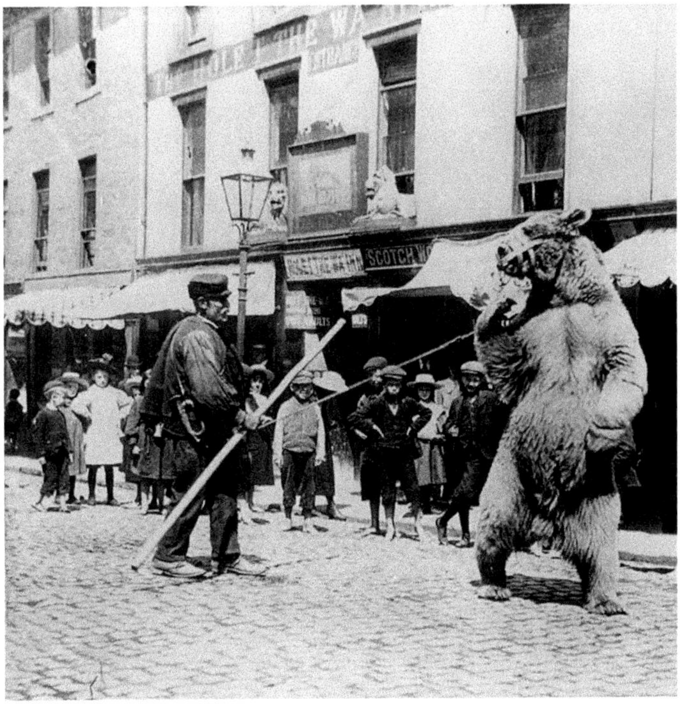

Dancing bear in the street, c. 1890.

> gentleman's watch in company what is the hour and minutes; he likewise tells any lady's thoughts in company, and distinguishes all sorts of colours.

Bisset died around 1785 and the pig, or more likely a replacement, was toured around Britain by a Mr Nicholson. The performance elicited debate about whether it proved pigs had special abilities or the pig was simply responding to prompting.

As more theatres opened, demand for animal acts grew. In 1819, audiences flocked to see Carlo, the celebrated dog from London:

> The dog will exhibit the following surprising feats. He is shot by an arrow, but recovers from the wound after his master has withdrawn the arrow. He seizes the dagger with which an Indian attempts to assassinate his master, and knocks from his master's hand the poisoned cup at the moment he raises it to his lips. He also releases his mistress who is tied to a tree by carrying a burning torch to her with which she burns her cords and escapes. Also attacks and kills a snake. With other supporting feats too numerous to mention.

Cats were not to be outshone. In 1831, Signor Cappelli, 'the Inimitable Tuscan', visited Edinburgh and exhibited his 'astonishing and sagacious cats' at a salon in Princes Street:

> These astonishing and well-tutored creatures will beat a drum! Turn a spit! Grind knives! Strike upon an anvil! Roast Coffee in the Italian manner; and other various exercises to the wonder of the spectators. Two of the cats (the cleverest of the company) will draw

> water out of a well at their master's command, without any other signal than the sound of the voice; this command being pronounced both in French and Italian.

Even one of the most reviled of creatures of the day was brought to the stage. Human flea circuses appeared in the early nineteenth century and were regular entertainments in Edinburgh. In 1881, Professor Ubini's Flea Circus was part of the annual carnival in Waverley Market:

> The insects have been trained to perform some astonishing feats by Professor Ubini who exhibits them. Four of the number who appear to be completely harnessed are engaged drawing a miniature mail coach, the coachman and guard, also fleas, being apparently dressed in Royal livery. Another exhibits Herculean strength for such a small insect by dragging about a model elephant 1,500 times its own weight, while another two are engaged in a duel with miniature swords. The fleas are well worth a visit, being interesting and amusing.

Flea circuses developed from jewellers and watchmakers displaying their skill by creating the miniature objects. The attraction continued into the early half of the twentieth century, but fortunately better hygiene and vacuum cleaners brought an end to these stage celebrities.

In 1894 the renowned Australian 'talking and thought reading horse', Mahomet, was presented at the Empire Palace by his owner and trainer, Mr Probasco:

> The horse, a handsome and well-groomed animal certainly displays remarkable intelligence in communicating information by means of gestures in reply to questions addressed to him by his master or the audience. Mahomet, if a question calls for

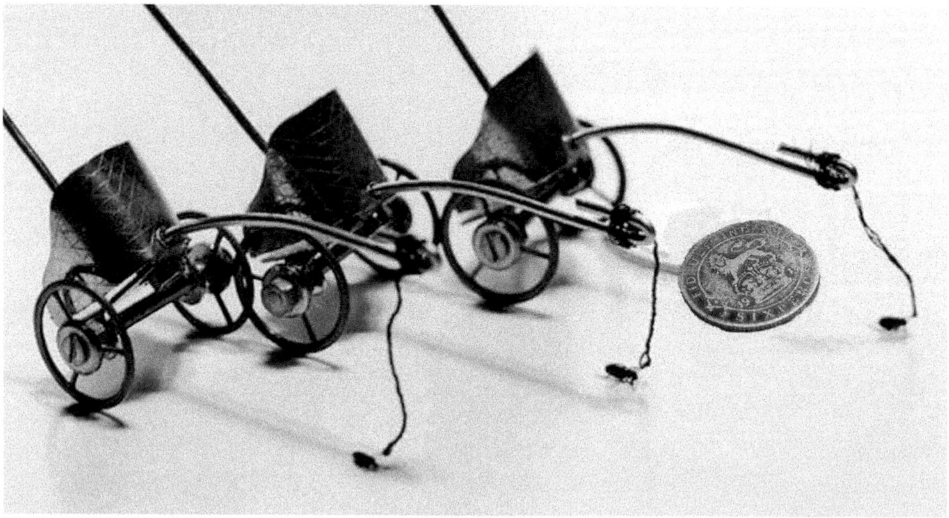

Flea circus 'chariots'.

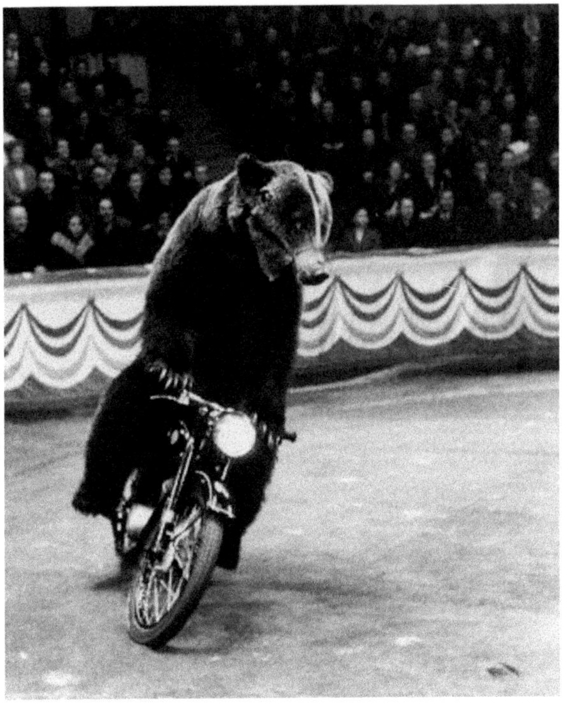

Bear riding a motorbike in a circus.

a negative reply, emphatically shakes his head, while he no less markedly nods if an affirmative is necessary. His readiness to answer questions put by Mr. Probasco in this manner having been demonstrated, some arithmetical tests were, by means of a blackboard, administered with great success. Figures being supplied by the audience and inscribed upon the board, Mahomet indicated, by scraping the floor of the stage with one of his forefeet, the correct answer to the problem put to him.

In the 1890s Mr Lavator's Dog Orchestra delighted city audiences. The six-strong band of mongrels performed on two drums, a violin, a bass and a trombone. Lavator expressed a pragmatic view of his canine musicians in an interview with *The Strand* magazine:

> I am uninterested in a dog's appearance as long as it is intelligent. I came up with the idea while performing in a circus in Denmark and began by buying a mongrel cheaply from the Copenhagen Dogs Home. But in spite of the dog becoming trained to beat a drum, it had to be replaced due to its pugnacious nature. Another of my dogs ran amok on a ferry and also had to be released, while a dog I trained as the trombonist had to be replaced as it had a tendency to leap off the stage into the audience.

It was the cats turn again in 1908. 'The Cat King', Leoni Clarke, brought his troupe of cats, rodents and canaries to the Waverley Market Carnival: 'One of the cats figures in a balloon descent, others leap through fiery hoops, and a number of the rodents are seen in a miniature railroad wreck. Cats walk over a rope of rats and mice and canaries, stepping

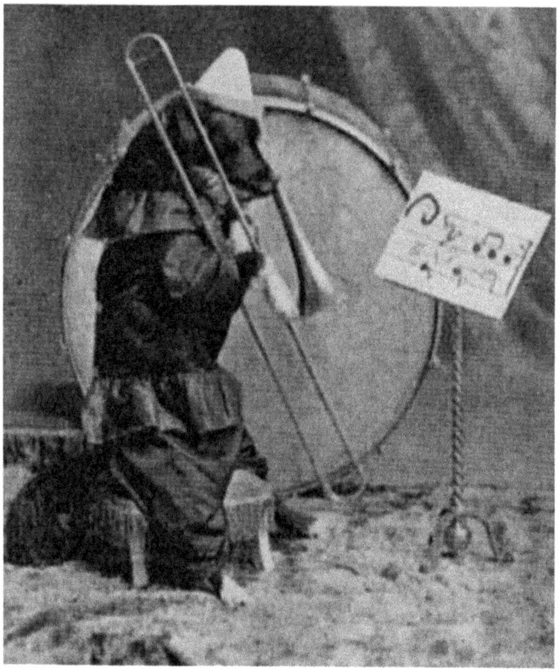

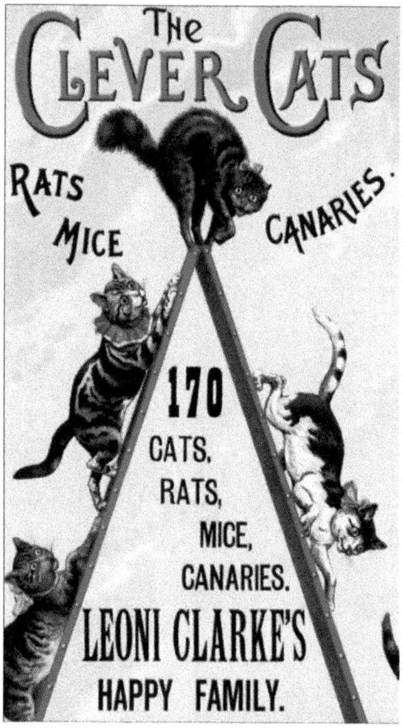

Above left: Trombonist dog in Lavator's Dog Orchestra, *c.* 1890

Above right: Poster for Leoni Clarke's Happy Family, *c.* 1908.

gingerly between the little fluttering bodies.' Clark told *The Scotsman* that he used around thirty cats in his act, but travelled with sixty or more. 'Cats are very skittish creatures', he said, 'and when they take the whim into their heads it is useless to take them on the stage.' Clarke explained that although he had trained all sorts of animals, from lions downwards, the most difficult of them all is the cat. 'A dog is sensible, a monkey accommodating, and a rat either forgives or forgets – but a cat! She is a hopeless bundle of sensibilities. Strike her once, if only by accident, and she will never perform again.' Clarke said the cat that climbed up a rope to the roof of the theatre and descended by parachute was the second that had done the trick as, he explained, 'The first became too fat and fell into bad ways.'

By 1900 the modern idea of a circus had begun to emerge. This combined equestrian acts, performing animals and other acts such as acrobats and clowns. In 1895, Wombwell's included 'The Wonderful Boxing Kangaroo, the champion of the world, worthy of the admission price alone.' One minister blamed such attractions for people no longer attending church: 'How could a man who had been watching the boxing kangaroo on Saturday night enjoy a discourse by a minister on Sunday morning?' However, two years earlier those who paid to see a boxing kangaroo at the Empire Palace Theatre were sorely disappointed: 'That a kangaroo should have boxing gloves fastened to its fore paws does not necessarily imply that it is a boxing kangaroo. The audience in the Empire Theatre last night expressed their disappointment with the melancholy exhibition made by the "timid animal" [so termed by its showman] that was carried round the ring while its

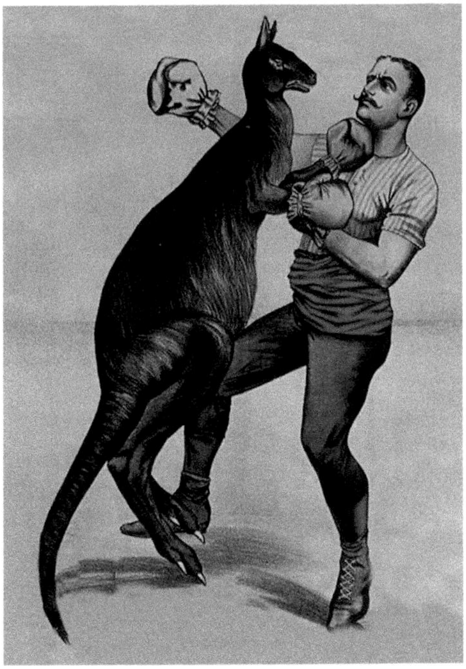

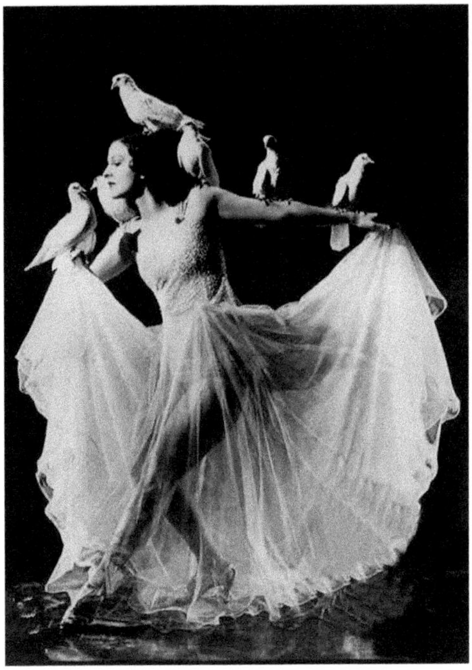

Above left: A boxing kangaroo.

Above right: Dancing with doves *c.* 1920.

gloves merely received repeated pats from the gloves of its antagonist. The second round ended with a storm of hisses.'

Prince's International Circus arrived in Edinburgh in December 1948 for performances in Waverley Market. The morning of its opening, Horbia Usem, a hypnotist, discovered that Sudan, one of his collaborators, was missing. This was a concern as Sudan was a 5-foot Nile crocodile largely made up of saw-toothed jaws and a powerful, lashing tail. All the circus employees swiftly began a search among the partly erected stands and booths and eventually found Sudan who, unused to Edinburgh's chill, had sensibly headed for the circus amphitheatre, which was being warmed for the comfort of the later audience. There he had settled down to sleep.

Many doves have been conjured out of nowhere on Edinburgh's stages over the years, but perhaps the most intriguing appearance was in Edna Squire-Brown's dance act. She toured Britain in the 1940s and 1950s and often appeared in Edinburgh. She was advertised as 'a dancer of international reputation' and one review said of her performance: 'A striking and artistic performance which cut away from conventional lines and which was enhanced by her use of a number of doves.' This may well have been an allusion to the genteel striptease that she performed. Her trained white doves fluttered above, only alighting on her whenever and wherever concealment was required. It is probably a myth that some young mischief-makers would attend her performances carrying packets of birdseed.

Rabbits also have appeared – or disappeared – many times in the city's theatres. In 2004, lots of the city's pet rabbits were excited when an opportunity to star in the Edinburgh Fringe arose. Jarrett & Raja, a magician and pianist, appealed to Edinburgh rabbit owners to lend their pets for an attempt to set a world record for pulling rabbits out of a hat. Around sixty-five rabbits (and their owners) turned up, but the bunnies' dreams of theatrical fame were dashed by concerns over the potential distress for the rabbits from the Scottish Society for the Prevention of Cruelty to Animals. 'It's a shame, because a lot of people came along and we had to say we couldn't use their rabbits,' said magician Jarrett Parker. 'We would never hurt any animal and all of the rabbits who took part today were very well cared for.' So the only rabbit to be conjured into stardom out of thin air that evening was the magician's own rabbit, Elvis.

Over the fifty-plus years of the Edinburgh Fringe, at least one goat has made it on stage. In 2019, a goat named Djali was among the cast in *Notre Dame de Paris* and for many in the audience upstaged the 12-metre-high representation of Notre Dame Cathedral that formed the set. While visiting the city Djali was taken for a ride on an Edinburgh bus and was delighted to be informed by the driver that on Lothian Buses goats travelled for free. No Fringe show is known to have featured a live sheep, although many have misled theatrical sheep aficionados by titles such as 'Black Sheep', 'Counting Sheep' and 'The Big Sheep'. However, in 2009 a lamb did appear on an Edinburgh stage. The Royal Lyceum Theatre gave Sam the Lamb his first acting role in the Sam Shephard play, *Curse of the Starving Class.* The lamb inserted various unscripted bleats during one scene and this may have resulted from a concern at the scene's content, which was an argument between two of the characters that leads to the lamb's demise.

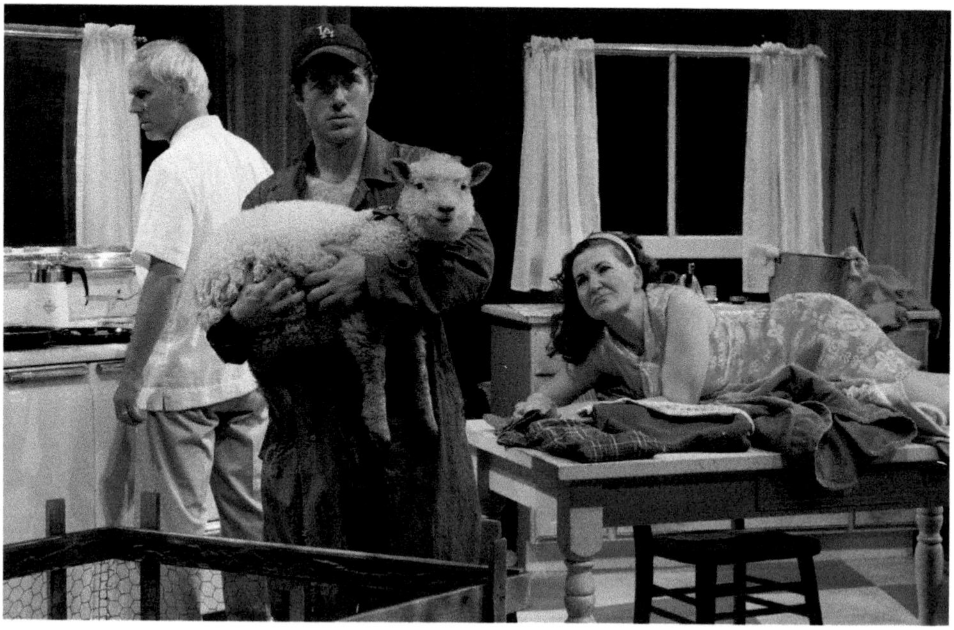

Lamb in *Curse of the Starving Class* by Sam Shephard. (Courtesy of Open Fist Theatre Company)

7. Dogs and Cats

Dr John Brown was an Edinburgh medical doctor, writer and lover of dogs. His most popular work was the 1859 short story about a dog, *Rab and His Friends*. Brown wrote why he believed every family should have a dog:

> It is like having a perpetual baby; it is the plaything and crony of the whole house. It keeps them all young. All unite upon the dog. He tells no tales, betrays no secrets, never sulks, asks no troublesome questions, never gets into debt, never comes down late for breakfast – is always ready for a bit of fun, lies in wait for it, and you may, if choleric, to your relief, kick him instead of someone else, who would not take it so meekly, and, moreover, would certainly not, as he does, ask your pardon for being kicked.

In a letter to a friend recounting the death of one of his favourite dogs, Brown wrote, 'Our darling little hairy terrier who got kicked and killed by a clumsy horse the other day because he was too good for this world, will certainly get between St Peter's legs as he lets

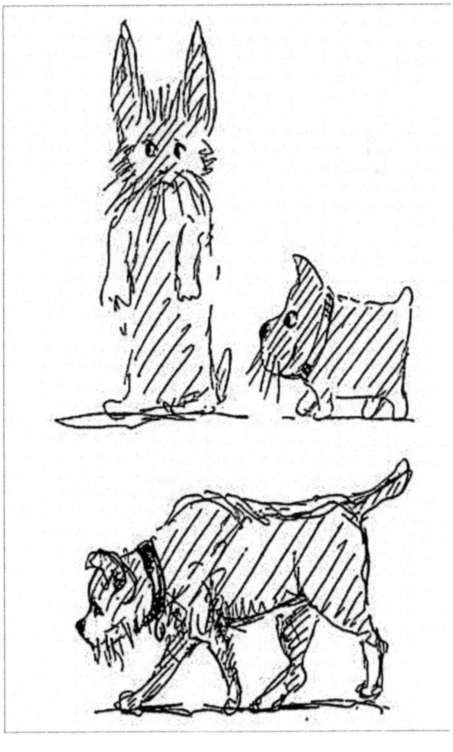

Drawings of his dogs by John Brown (1810–82).

me in. Meantime, keep happy, and let us both look for the happy hunting-ground where we shall meet all our dogs again.' Robert Louis Stevenson echoed Brown's view on dogs entering the pearly gates: 'You think those dogs will not be in heaven! I tell you they will be there long before any of us.'

Dogs belonging to many Edinburgh owners have got lost over the centuries. Adverts in the eighteenth century seeking the return of strayed dogs often were substantial and their cost indicated their owners regard for their pet. One in 1761 was common of the type:

> Stolen or Strayed on 24th of this month, between four and five afternoon, from Mr Peter Ramsay's at the Red Lyon without the Cowgate Port. A Little Black Lap Dog, of King Charles's breed, very long ears, white breast, the hair of his neck a little ruffled with a collar, answers to the name of Joba, his tail is very short, occasioned by its being cut when young. Whoever finds him, and brings him to Lieutenant Warran of General Holmes's regiment, now quartered in the Castle, shall receive half a guinea reward, and no questions will be asked.

Later that year, when Captain Raines Sutherland advertised for the return of his pointer, his advert added to the offer of a handsome reward a threat: 'If the dog is not returned, and found in the possession of any person, such person will be held as the thief, and will be prosecuted with the utmost rigour of the law.'

In earlier times there were large numbers of stray dogs and in 1738, in response to the rise in deaths from rabies due to dog bites, Edinburgh magistrates ordered all owners to

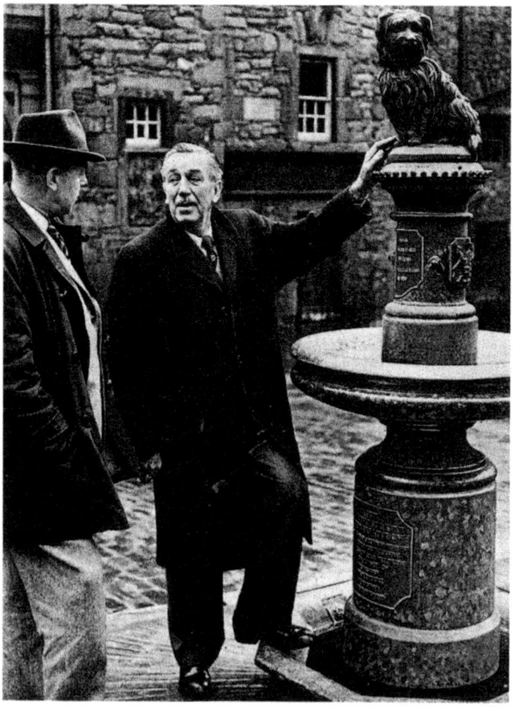

Walt Disney visiting Greyfriars Bobby statue prior to making a film of Bobby's life (1960).

remove their dogs from the city for at least a month so that stray dogs could be killed. The city guard were offered a reward of 1*s* for each dog dispatched and such was their zeal that they killed 'even the dogs that lead the blind about the streets'. In 1796, the government introduced a dog tax. Prior to its introduction there had been strong arguments for and against the idea. Many landowners were in favour as they believed it would reduce poaching by discouraging dog ownership amongst the poor, while others simply thought that poor people who could barely feed themselves should not keep a dog as a pet. The initial tax was 5*s* per sporting or hunting dog, such as greyhounds and spaniels, and 3*s* for working dogs. (The weekly wage of a labourer at this time was about 5*s*.) The dog tax rolls for 1797 record payment for 366 dogs in Edinburgh. Baron Norton, a judge, who lived at Abbeyhill paid tax on twenty-nine working dogs – probably a pack of hunting hounds.

In 1867, the dog tax was replaced by a dog licence at an increased fee of 7*s* 6*d* and it was this that brought Greyfriars Bobby to public notice. The man who fed the stray Bobby over many of the years the dog had been visiting his dead master's grave was asked to pay but declined. Instead, Sir William Chambers, the Lord Provost, paid for Bobby's licence and presented him with a collar with a brass inscription: 'Greyfriars Bobby from the Lord Provost 1867 licensed.' After Bobby died in 1872, Baroness Burdett-Coutts, President of the Ladies Committee of the RSPCA, was so deeply moved by his story that she paid for the granite fountain and statue of Bobby. Unusually, the city council decided that Bobby could be buried in Greyfriars Kirk graveyard although normally regulations did not allow animals to be interred in the city's human cemeteries.

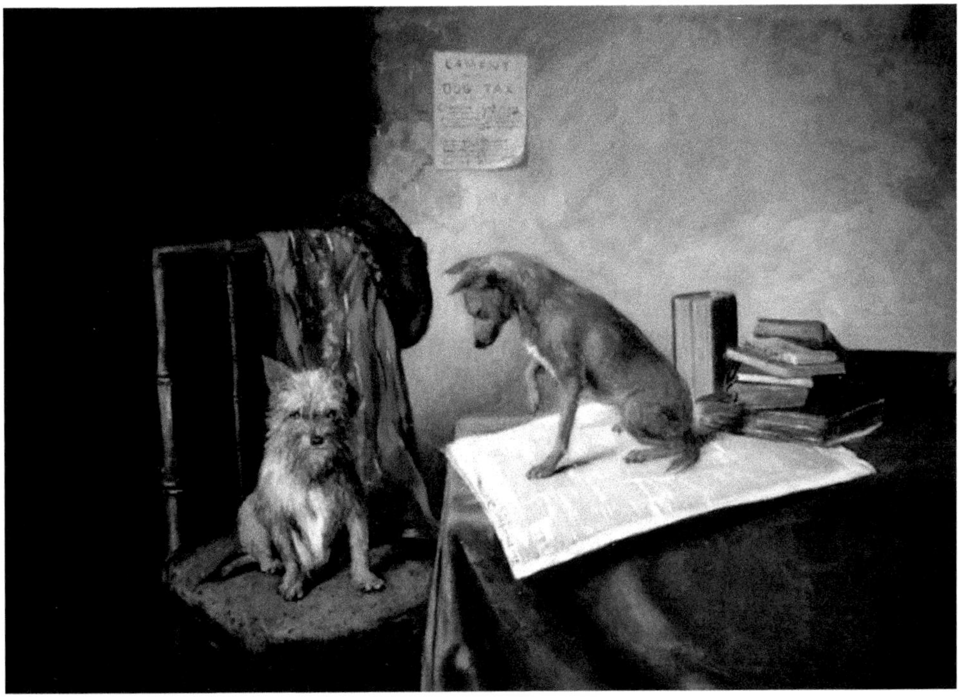

Lament on the Dog Tax by William Geddes (1840–84).

The only other dog to be interred in a city cemetery was buried in Piershill Cemetery in 1911. She was a pit bull terrier named Beauty and the favourite pet of Sigmund Neuberger, a famous German magician who performed as the Great Lafayette. Beauty had been given to him by his fellow magician, Harry Houdini. On 30 April 1911, Lafayette travelled to Edinburgh to perform at the Empire Palace (now the Festival Theatre) and the day after he arrived Beauty unexpectedly died. Lafayette was grief-stricken and sought permission to bury his dog in one of the city's cemeteries. The council eventually agreed on condition that when Lafayette died he would be buried in the same grave. Lafayette agreed. During this extended negotiation Beauty had been embalmed and placed inside an expensive oak coffin, and was lying in an Edinburgh undertaker's chapel of rest awaiting her funeral on 10 May. The evening before, Lafayette was on stage performing his final illusion, 'The Lion's Bride'. Disastrously, a lantern set fire to part of the set and the blaze swiftly spread. The fire curtain was dropped and while all the audience escaped unscathed, Lafayette, ten other performers and stagehands, a lion and a horse died.

The magician's body was removed from the wreckage, cremated and the ashes placed in an expensive urn. The following day, a further body was discovered in the stage debris and identified as Lafayette by his diamond rings. The earlier body had been his stage double! On 14 May, the urn, now containing the correct ashes, and Beauty's coffin were taken to Piershill Cemetery. The funeral was a vast affair with over 100,000 people lining the route. At the cemetery the urn containing the ashes of the Great Lafayette was placed in Beauty's coffin between her two outstretched paws and interred.

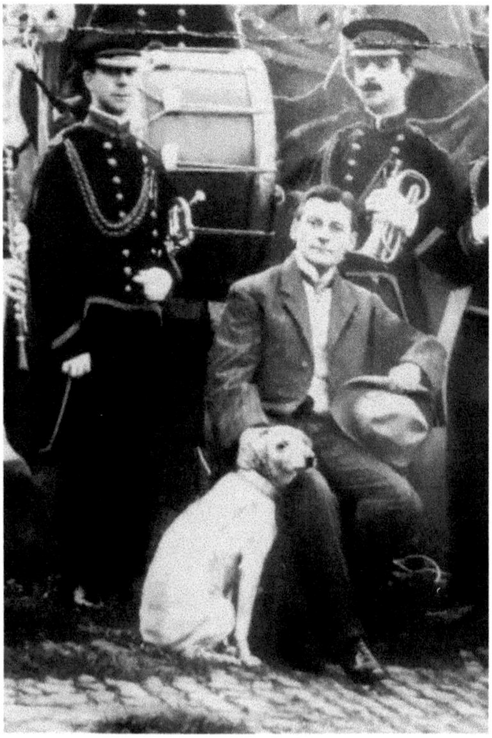

Sigmund Neuberger (The Great Lafayette) and his dog Beauty, *c.* 1905.

Inside Edinburgh Castle there is a dog cemetery where dogs with links to Scottish regiments are buried. It is thought that the first to be buried there was the castle's commanding officer's dog, Fido, in 1847. One dated 1887 commemorates Pat, the regimental mascot of the 72nd Highlanders (later the Seaforth Highlanders) who travelled with the regiment in campaigns in Afghanistan and Egypt.

William Kingston's *Stories of Animal Sagacity*, published in 1875, recounted many stories of clever animals including one smart Edinburgh dog:

> In the 1820s Dugald M'Intyre, a patent-mangle manufacturer who lived in the Canongate owned a dog called Dandie. The dog was well-known in the neighbourhood for its intelligence, and most days someone would give the dog a penny, which he carried in his mouth to the baker's shop, and exchanged for bread which he ate. One day a man who often gave the dog its penny was approached by Dandie in expectation of his usual present. The man, having no pennies on him, said to the dog, 'I have not a penny with me to-day, but I have one at home.' Having returned to his house later, a noise was heard at the door and when the servant opened it, in sprang Dandie seeking his penny. As a jest the man gave Dandie a bad one which the dog, as usual, carried to the baker, but there was refused his bread as the money was bad. Dandie immediately returned to the man's house and when the door was opened at his clawing, laid the bad penny down at the servant's feet and strode off, seemingly with the greatest contempt.

The National Portrait Gallery in Queen Street owes its existence to a dog. In 1895, James Cowan Smith, a Scottish-born civil engineer, commissioned John Emms, a respected artist who specialised in paintings of dogs and horses, to paint a portrait of his Dandie Dinmont, a breed of terrier, called Callum. Smith was a philanthropist and left a bequest of more than £55,000 (£2,500,000 today) to the National Gallery of Scotland to be used to expand its collections. His bequest was made with two unusual conditions: the first

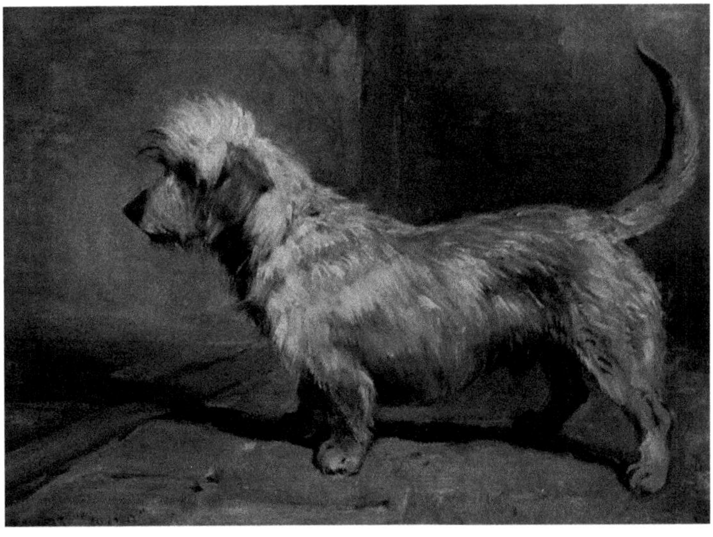

Portrait of the Dandie Dinmont by John Emms, 1888.

that the gallery cared for his dog Fury, who survived him; the second that the painting of Callum should always be permanently displayed; Callum still graces the walls of the gallery.

Edinburgh's famous caricaturist John Kay was a cat lover and in his 1786 self-portrait Kay depicts himself with a bust of the Greek poet Homer and his painting utensils on the table. He sits in a large chair and curled on its back is his large pet cat, which he believed to be the biggest in Scotland. Kay was originally a barber and a later hairdresser, John Sturrock, also owned a large cat, named Tom. It lived in his Princes Street salon to ward off mice and during the day would lie asleep in the window. Sturrock was 'Hair-Dresser & Perfumer to Her Majesty in ordinary for Scotland' and in 1870 Alfred, the second son of Queen Victoria, visited Sturrock to have his hair cut. Alfred was so taken by Tom that he asked to borrow the impressive tomcat to show to the Princess of Wales and her children. From that day on Sturrock's cat was nicknamed 'Royal Tom', although being fourteen and half at the time of his Holyrood Palace visit, his royal accolade was short-lived. However, Royal Tom was later memorialised in the *Chatterbox Album of Animals.*

In 1871, Edinburgh's first Scottish Metropolitan Cat Show was held and around 300 cats were exhibited in forty categories, including blue tabbies, short-haired whites and the 'largest cat of any sex'. The latter category was won by the hefty 24-pound cat belonging to Mrs Clarke of Drummond Place. *The Scotsman*'s report on the show began:

> The cat undoubtedly takes the premier place in the list of our domestic pets. Many people keep tabbies as useful vermin hunters, others from a soft-hearted benevolence; some

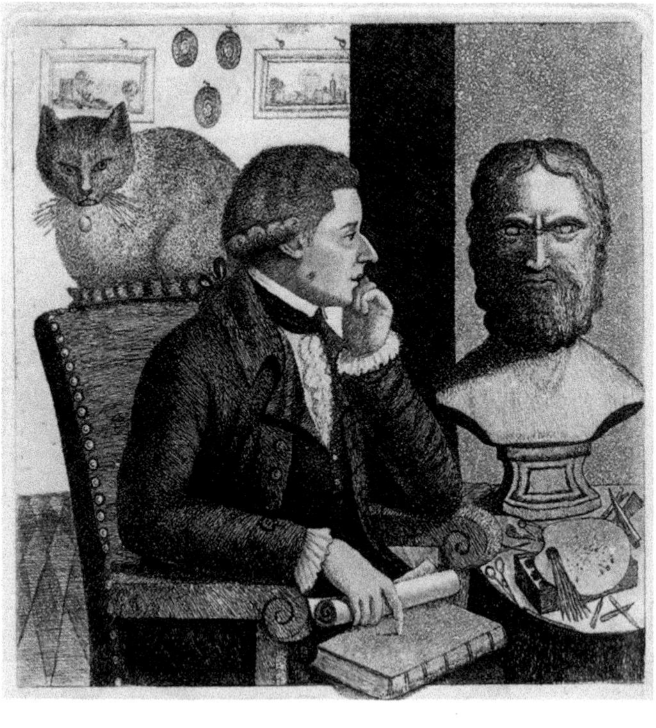

Self-portrait with cat by John Kay (1786).

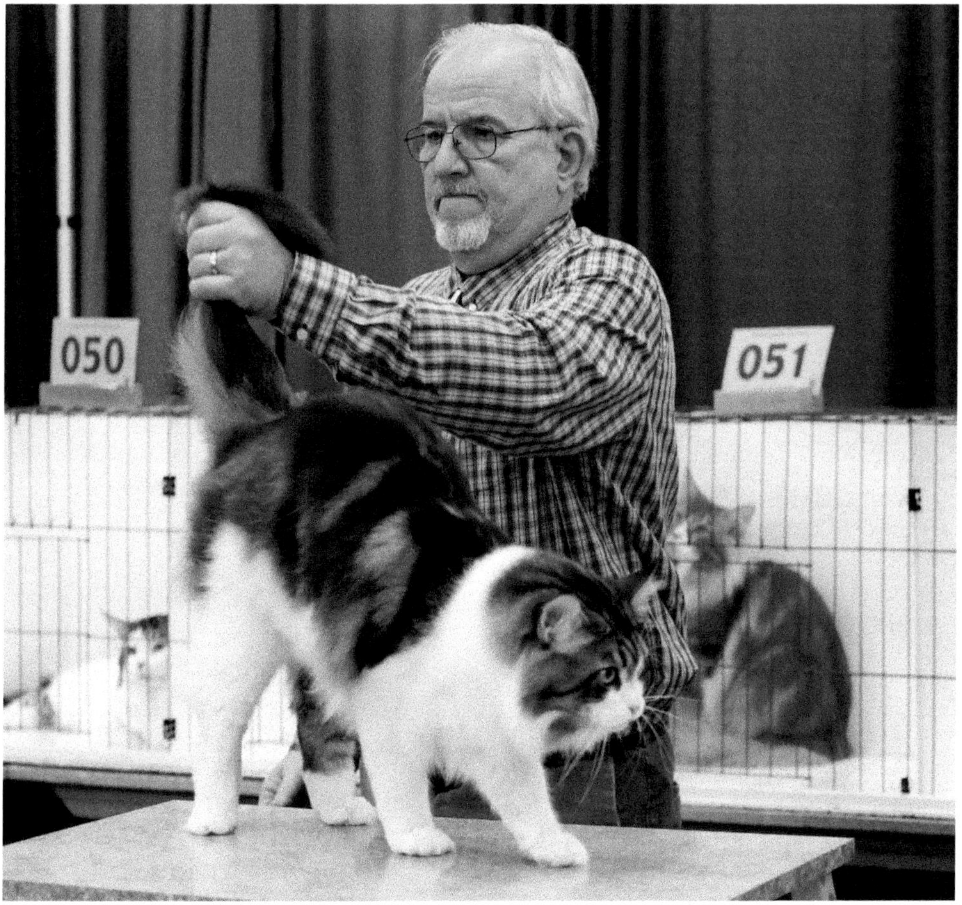

Cat show. (Courtesy of Jill Carlson under Creative Commons)

> from custom and others from the instinctive love of animals which is said to be inherent in the breasts of all mankind ... Even to those who care little for cats, it is astonishing what an interesting exhibition the array makes. Here is the spinster's guide philosopher and friend, there the child's playful pet. In the next cage one that is spoiled and overfed, and beyond that the demure tabby.

Dogs were exhibited as part of shows of horses, cattle, etc., but in 1864 the first Scottish dog show was held in Glasgow and in 1871 'The First Waverley Dog Show' was held in Edinburgh. The following year the show was renamed the Scottish Metropolitan Dog Show and took place over three days at the Royal Patent Gymnasium. The gymnasium had been built six years earlier on the site of the drained Canonmill Loch and was more like a funfair, offering a variety of attractions, including the 'Great Sea Serpent', a 600-person rowing machine. Over 700 dogs were entered and were 'mostly all of a very high standard, indeed, greatly superior to those of last time'. Hunting dogs such as deerhounds, greyhounds, fox terriers and retrievers were deemed 'the first division'; while 'the second division' included terriers, Newfoundlands, collies and puppies.

If Edinburgh's earlier writers and artists often focused on the dog, in recent years Edinburgh has been home to two of the most gifted portrayers of cats. Elizabeth Blackadder's paintings of cats are much admired and in 1995 Royal Mail used images of six of her cat paintings on a set of postage stamps. The writer Aileen Paterson created the memorable children's books featuring Maisie Mackenzie, a Morningside kitten. Dressed in a kilt and Fair Isle jumper, Maisie undertakes a range of adventures in a world without humans or dogs, and while the characters are mainly cats, a belligerent budgie and the occasional horse also feature.

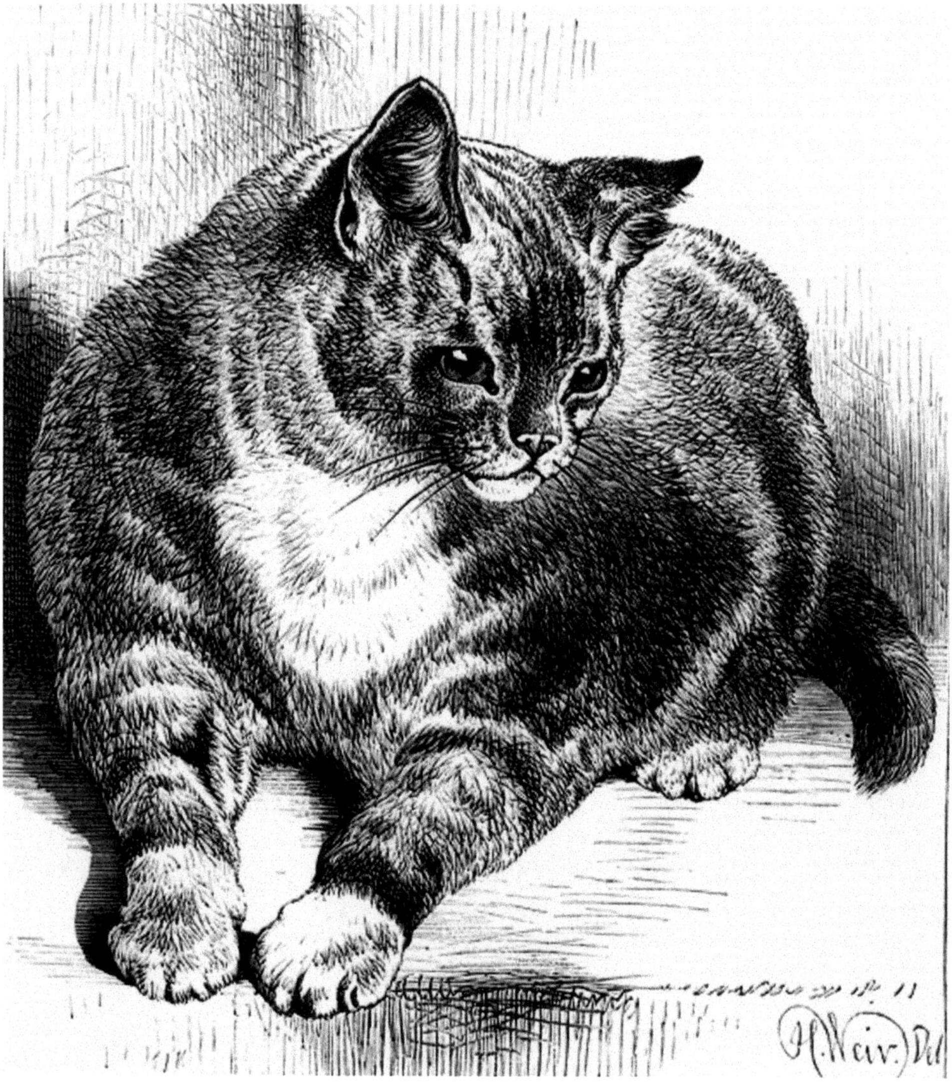

Royal Tom by Harrison Weir from *Chatterbox Album of Animals* (1880).

8. Food and Fashion

The Cowgate takes its name from the medieval practice of herding cattle down the street on market days – 'gate' being a Scots word for 'way' or 'road' – and for many centuries the cattle market was in Grassmarket. While the poor in medieval times, and later, lived on a diet of barley, oatmeal, curly kale and cabbage, supplemented by a rare scrap of pork, beef or mutton, large numbers of cattle and sheep were brought to the city for slaughter to feed the wealthier residents. The amount the richest people consumed is hinted at by an estimate made by Alexia Soyer, a celebrated Victorian chef, of the animals he would eat in his lifetime. This included 30 oxen, 200 sheep, 100 calves, 200 lambs, 50 pigs; 1,200 chickens, 300 turkeys, 150 geese, 400 ducklings, 263 pigeons; 2,500 game birds, 500 hares and rabbits, 40 deer, 120 guinea fowl, 10 peacocks, 3,500 fish and 350,000 crustaceans.

Edinburgh's Guild of Fleshers (butchers) was incorporated in 1488 and until the mid-nineteenth century many of the city's abattoirs and meat markets were located on the edges of the Old Town – hence street names such as Fleshmarket Close. In 1642, the town council ruled that the fleshers 'shall provide themselves of sufficient slaughter houses outside the burgh or at the North Loch ... and shall not cast forth any blood or filth upon

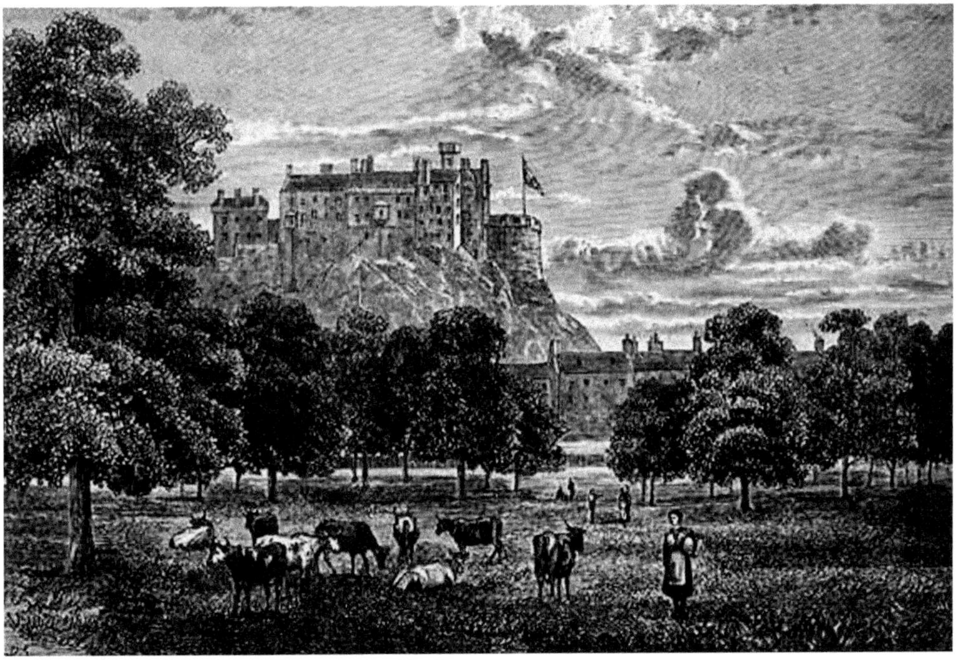

Cattle grazing on the meadows, *c.* 1800. (Courtesy of Old and New Edinburgh)

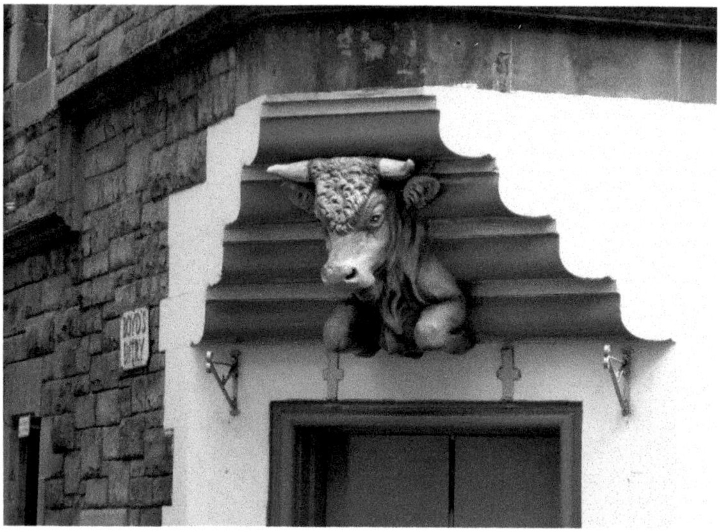

Old butcher's shop sign in Edinburgh.

the streets or vennels'. The effluent from the slaughtering then flowed into the North Loch. The fleshers clearly were a coarse crowd. The 1673 regulations included a ban on 'driving beasts on the Sabbath under penalty of £5'; a control against the 'fleshers and their servants frequent swearing and cursing' with a fine of 6*s* for each oath; and as 'fleshers are known to keep seven or eight dogs' a restriction to 'two dogs for driving cattle and one for sheep'.

In 1817, a writer to the *Caledonian Mercury* protested at the way animals were being slaughtered: 'The horrid and inhuman use of the axe in slaughtering cattle is a disgrace to the characteristic humanity of the British nation.' In 1852, the health risks of animals being butchered near residences led to the opening of the city's first municipal slaughterhouse in Fountainbridge and more humane methods of slaughter evolved. The cattle market moved to Lauriston Place in 1843 and in 1900 part was demolished to make way for a new central fire station, with resulting conflict between dawdling cows and speeding fire engines.

Pigs that were kept in the city roamed the streets looking for scraps and in 1670 the council ordered that no swine should be allowed 'to come upon the high street or in any close or vennel ... and any found upon the streets shall be confiscated'. Yet a few pigs were still loose on the streets in the 1750s as the young Duchess of Gordon and her sister rode down the Royal Mile on the back of two belonging to the proprietor of the Red Lion Inn, although it was said that these 'were not the common vagrants of the High Street, but belonged to Peter Ramsay and were among the last swine that were allowed to roam abroad'.

Although cows did not roam the streets, a large number were kept within the city. Fresh milk was sold from the shops of cow keepers (also known as cow feeders) that were dotted around the city until milk deliveries became common. Some New Town houses had their own small byres at the rear where a single cow could be kept. The existence of cowsheds in populated areas was a significant health risk and in 1900 there were still 115 licensed cowsheds within the city, containing around 3,000 cows.

The name of Old Fishmarket Close refers to when it was the central fishmarket. In 1684, town council minutes record 'that all persons bringing fishes to the city take the

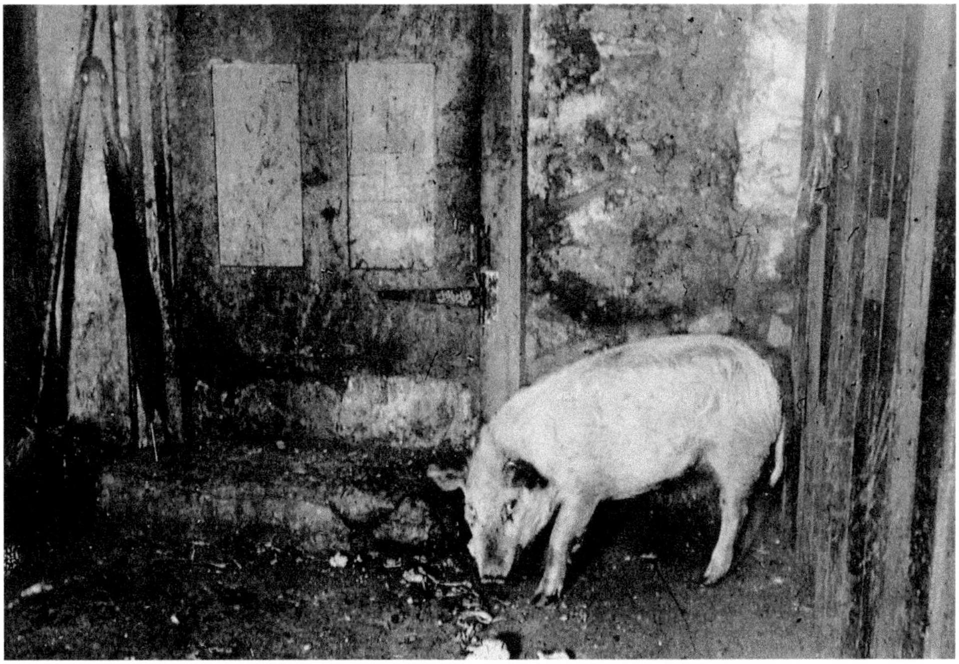

Pig in street. (Courtesy of Jacob A Riis under Creative Commons)

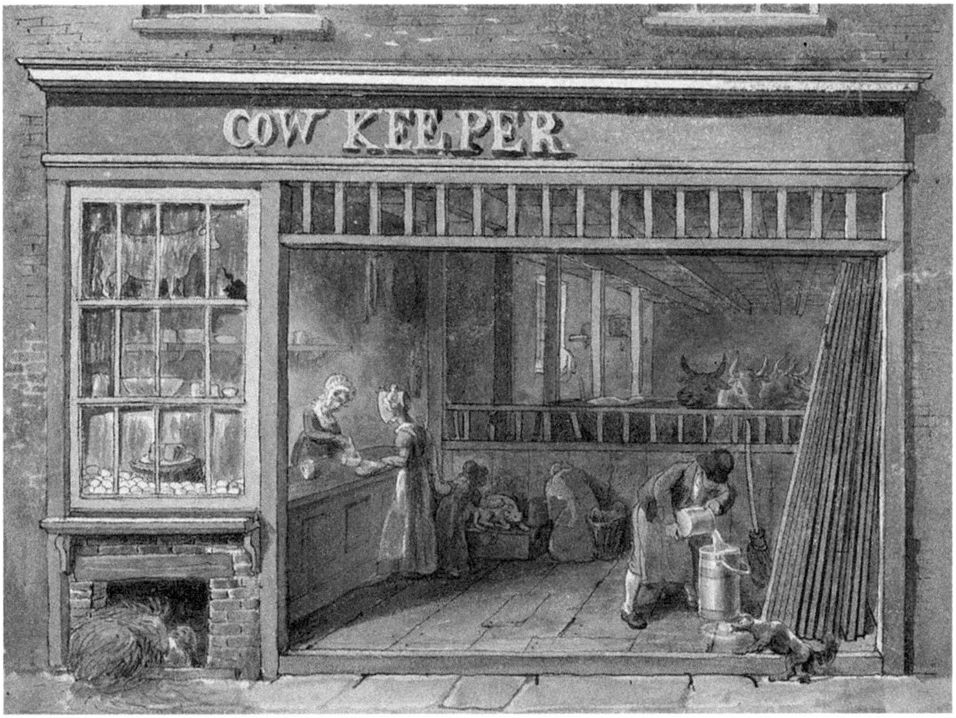

Cowkeeper by George the Elder Scharf, 1852.

same to the new fishmarket to be sold excepting oysters and other shell fishes which are commonly cried through the streets'. Oysters once were widely consumed by Edinburgh's rich and poor. Fisherwomen would bring the fresh oysters into the city, announcing their presence with the cry of 'Caller ou' (Caller oysters). So many were eaten that empty oyster shells were widely available and local stonemasons used them as a handy way of packing joints – many can still be seen in ancient buildings in the Old Town.

While there are still stories nowadays of contaminated food, the meat and fish being sold in Edinburgh in Victorian times was more often than not of dubious quality. An 1892 report stated that in the previous year over 375,000 pounds of diseased meat and fish had been seized or prevented from being put on sale by the sanitary officers.

Bull, cow, sheep, pig and other animal skins were in great demand, as Edinburgh was a centre for leather production from the fifteenth century on. The animal hides came from the city's slaughterhouses or were imported. Demand for shoes, boots, gloves, saddles, harnesses and other objects, such as snuffboxes, led to more tanneries; as the process was unpleasant and smelly, most of these were based on the outskirts.

Large numbers of bird feathers also were needed. In 1787, an advert in the *Caledonian Mercury* announced: 'To the Ladies. The Ostrich Feather Manufactory is removed from St Andrew's Street to the Assembly Rooms, George Street where ladies and others may be

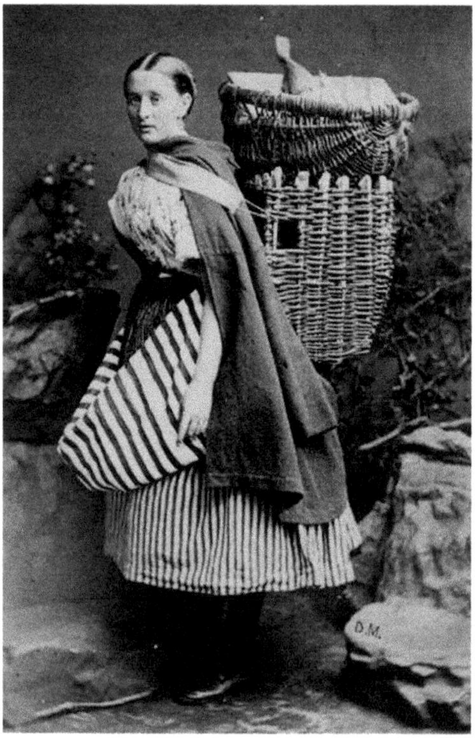

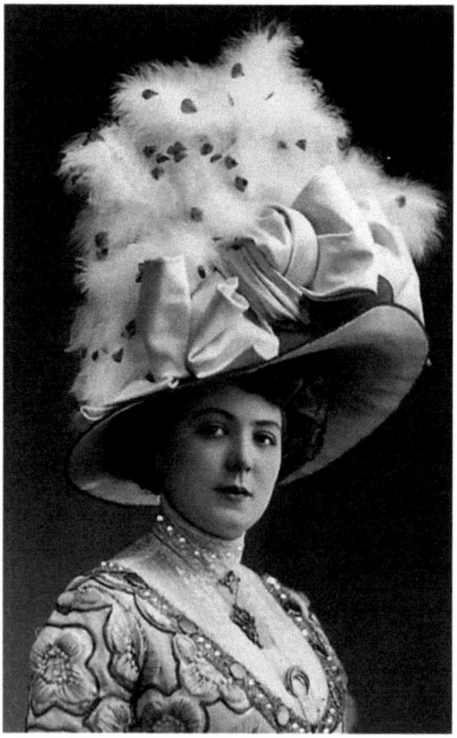

Above left: Newhaven fishwife, *c*. 1910.

Above right: Woman wearing hat with feathers *c*. 1910.

supplied on reasonable terms.' Ostrich feathers, long used on military hats, became much sought after by fashionable women in Victorian times and a dramatic plume of black ostrich feathers on the horses pulling funeral carriages was an essential fashion item for the deceased wealthy. The considerable demand was bad news for ostriches, as they were almost hunted to extinction before being saved by the innovation of ostrich farms in South Africa in the 1860s.

Other birds were not so fortunate. By the 1880s Britain was importing exotic plumes from all over the globe, including from species as diverse as birds of paradise, hummingbirds, storks, vultures, ibises, toucans and parrots. The order of one London dealer alone included 6,000 bird of paradise feathers, 40,000 hummingbird feathers and 360,000 feathers from various East Indian species. Feathers from native birds such as herons, kingfishers and owls were also being 'harvested' for the fashion industry. In the 1880s, the Plumage League was established to campaign to outlaw the killing of birds for their feathers and a letter published in *The Scotsman* in 1865 supported the idea:

> Having read with interest the article on the Plumage League, I trust some further steps may be taken to put a stop to the barbarous slaughter of beautiful birds. Women are by no means heartless and few I think fully grasp the idea of the many hundreds of songsters that must be yearly sacrificed on the altar of fashion for their gratification. But why do not the men openly set their faces against it? If they did few women would, I believe, ornament their hats with feathers at the cost of so many joyous lives.

In 1891, the Society for the Protection of Birds was established and thirty years later the first act prohibiting the importation of specific feathers was introduced. An advert in 1892 listing racoon, lynx, beaver, bear, leopard, kangaroo, tiger, opossum, skunk, seal, mink, wolverine, fox and otter might appear to be for a menagerie or zoo, but was actually advertising fur coats and other garments. For those who could not afford the more expensive furs, coats were available made from cheaper skins such as weasel, squirrel or mole, and even rabbit skin dyed to look like a more expensive fur. The use of fur in clothing was long employed by royalty as a symbol of wealth and social status, and from Victorian times on massive imports fed the rising fashion for fur among both women and men. A Jewish man named Philip Levy established one of the earliest fur manufacturers in Edinburgh in 1818, and by the 1840s advertised himself as 'Fur manufacturer to Her Majesty of Scotland'. In 1860, he was granted a Royal Letters Patent for his invention of 'an improved wrapper for travelling and personal wear, whereby the Feet as well as the Knees are constantly kept warm and comfortable'. These later were advertised as 'Railway and carriage wrappers' and were no doubt much appreciated on lengthy draughty journeys.

From the 1870s Marcus in Princes Street was one of the main fur shops. Above its entrance were three bears that sadly were thrown away when the building was redeveloped. In the 1890s there was a fashion for fur neck-pieces, but the *Edinburgh Evening News* was unimpressed: 'Fair ladies now walk about with entire fur-coated creatures tied around their necks – glittering eyes, pointed nose and ears, four tiny feet, small tail and all. It is not a pretty idea thus to have stripped an animal of its outer covering and to wear the fur *au naturel* round the throat.'

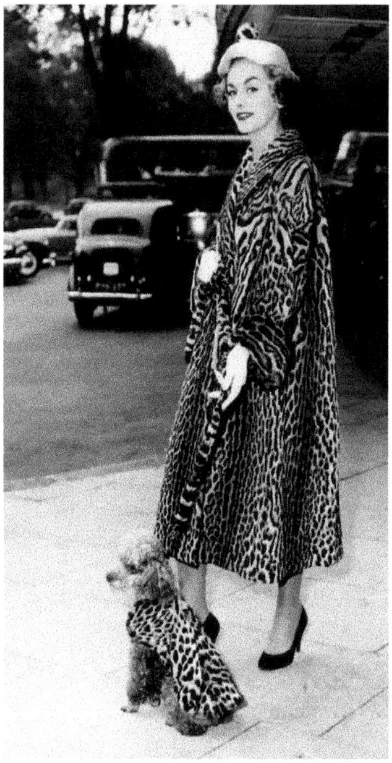

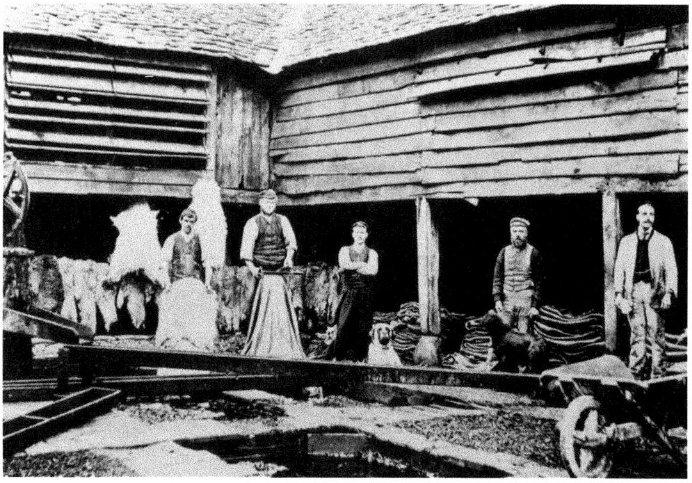

Above: Tannery, *c.* 1900.

Left: Matching leopard coats, *c.* 1930.

Fashion also demanded supplies of whalebone – in fact the fibrous substance that grows on the baleen plates in the mouths of certain whales to strain sea food from the water – as its flexibility and strength made it a vital component in the production of the corsets that created the narrow waists on women that fashion required. The material also kept Edinburgh's lums clean as chimney sweeps' brushes were made from it.

It was not only animal skins for clothing that were imported into the city. In the heyday of the Empire, Scots were slaying wild animals across the world for sport and many were shipped back to Scotland as trophies. In 1860, a grand dinner was held in Edinburgh's Corn Exchange to welcome the 78th Highlanders home from India:

> The room was splendidly and appropriately decorated with rare, ancient, or valuable military and hunting trophies lent from gentlemen in various parts of the country, admirably displayed by the light of gas ... The centrepiece was the dark hide of a splendid yak, or wild bull of Chinese Tartary, which had fallen under the rifle of Colonel Dewar; and around it were grouped a magnificent lion's skin with head and tusks preserved, and skins of tigers, leopards, and other eastern animals.

By the 1980s the first stirrings of protest at wearing fur began to emerge. In 1984, members of the Animal Liberation Front smashed the windows of Dominion Furs in Morningside and the business closed soon after. The debate about the use of animal skins has particular resonance in Scotland for one significant use has been in the production of sporrans. In 2007, the Scottish government introduced legislation to protect endangered species whose skins had been traditionally popular with sporran manufacturers.

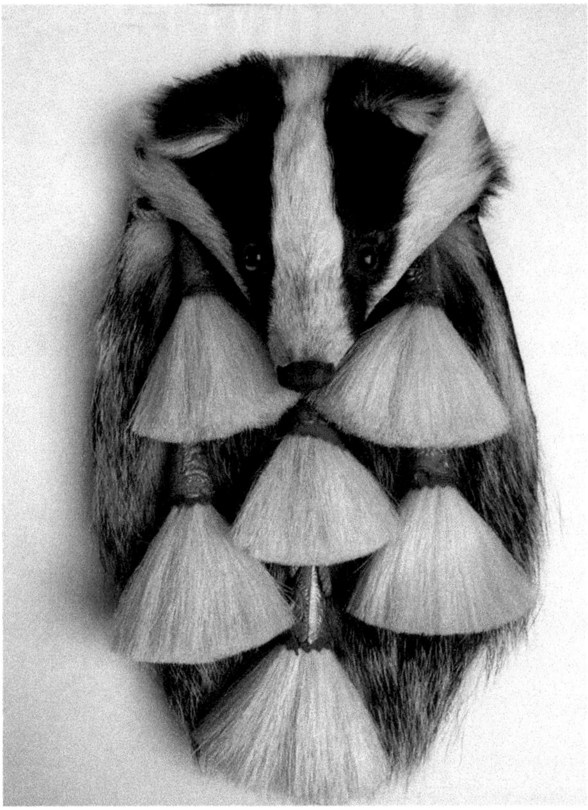
A badger sporran.

Before 1800 the number of beehives in Scotland was relatively small. James Bonner, a weaver, kept beehives, and in his spare time carried out research and experimentation to improve his beekeeping. To supplement his low wages as a weaver Bonner sold honeycombs and in 1794, while taking some of his fine honeycombs to a buyer, was stopped by a gentleman who asked if he could buy some. The next day Bonner arrived at the man's house in the New Town to discover his new buyer was Sir John Sinclair, a British politician, writer on agriculture and president of the Royal Highland and Agricultural Society of Scotland. Sinclair quizzed Bonner about his beekeeping and was so impressed that he arranged for the Highland Society to provide support so that Bonner could write a treatise on the subject. In 1795, Bonner published *A New Plan for Speedily Increasing the Number of Bee-hives in Scotland*, which was influential in expanding the keeping of bees.

Hens were widely kept to provide fresh eggs, and one Edinburgh hen outdid all others in the city during the 1940s. She hatched on 10 April 1939 at Edinburgh's Institute of Animal Genetics Poultry Research Centre and was given the somewhat prosaic title of Chicken L1641. Oblivious to the onset of the Second Word War L1641 laid her first egg later that year. Over the next eight years L1641 produced 1,515 eggs, matching the world record for egg production by a single hen. Sadly, she died in the autumn of 1948, missing out on world fame by just one egg.

9. Uncommon Pets

While dogs and cats have always been the most usual pets among Edinburgh's residents, other animals have had their admirers. In the 1750s a piglet that was roaming the city's streets in search of scraps took a liking to Lord Gardenstone who was walking back to his Canongate house. The piglet followed the learned judge home and Gardenstone was so taken with the pig's devotion that he took it in as a pet. The lord became so fond of his piglet that he permitted it to share his bed. When the pig grew to its adult size this sleeping arrangement became awkward and although Gardenstone evicted the animal from his bed, he allowed it to share his bedroom. Houses in the old town were chilly in winter and when Gardenstone undressed in the cold months he laid his clothes on the floor for the pig to lie on for, as he explained, this arrangement meant his clothes were warm in the morning.

In the 1770s the once fashionable and beautiful Lady Eglintoune who was much sought after by Edinburgh's nobility and gentry in her youth, amused herself in old age by taming rats. She jested that she had never met with true gratitude except from four-footed animals. Her ladyship had a panel in the oak wainscot of her dining room, and when she opened it at mealtimes, a dozen white rats appeared and joined her at table. At a signal from her ladyship the well-fed rats obediently scurried back through the panel.

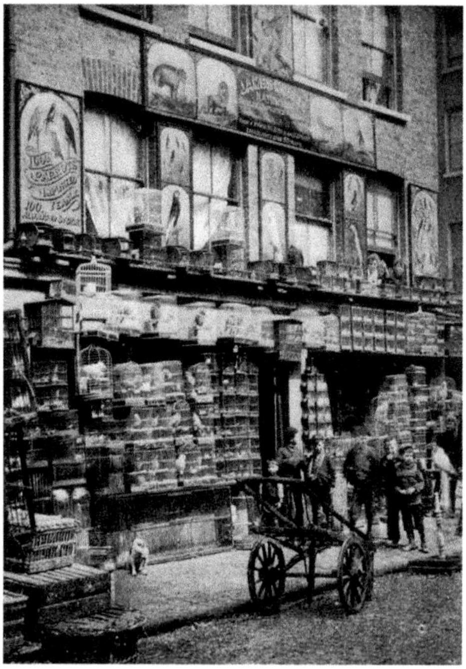

Pet shop, *c.* 1890.

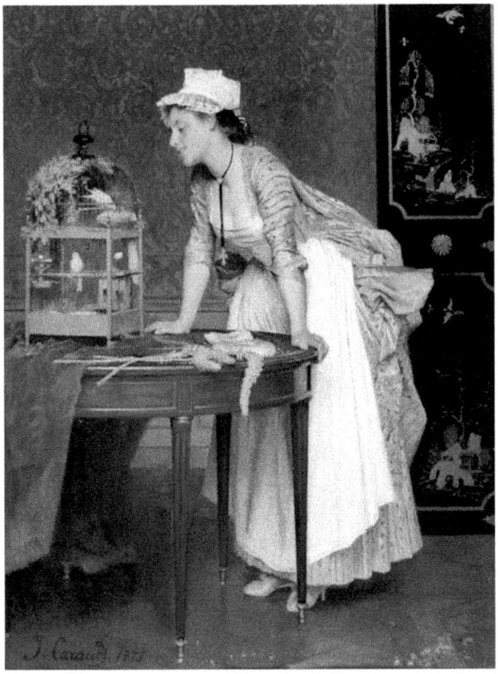

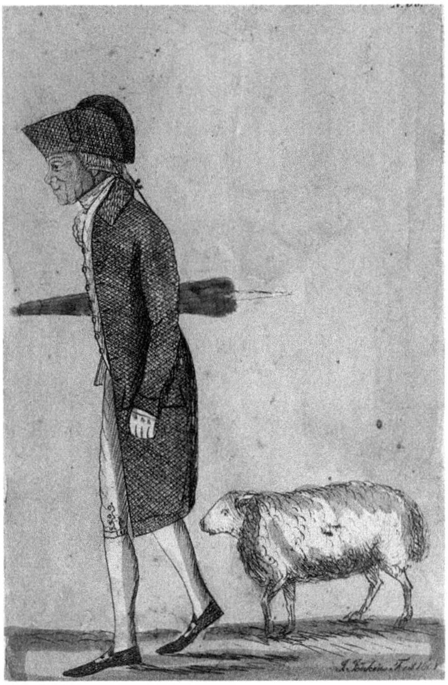

Above left: *The Pet Canaries* by Joseph Caraud, 1875.

Above right: Dr Wood and his pet sheep, Sandy. (From *Edinburgh Characters* by J. Jenkins, National Library of Scotland)

More understandable was the keeping of caged songbirds such as skylarks, goldfinches and the like for their especially melodious songs. In the seventeenth century canaries began to be imported by British royalty and Mrs Bellamy, an Edinburgh actor in the 1750s, owned a large collection of these singing birds. She insisted that her many cages of birds shared her dressing room in whatever theatre she was performing in and even arranged for them to be transported to Glasgow when she performed there. The wealthier often kept private aviaries, and James Burnett, an Edinburgh stationer, had one on the roof of his house in Hermitage Brae. This was perhaps unwise as it was a wire cage and one day in 1832 it was struck by lightning during a storm, and all the birds were killed.

Dr Wood, nicknamed Lang Sandy as he was tall and slim, lived in York Place in the 1770s and owned a pet sheep called Willy. As his house lacked a garden he arranged for Willy to graze in the garden outside Dundas House in St Andrew Square. Each day Wood would collect Willy and take him on his visits to patients. If no suitable grazing area was available outside the sheep would be taken into the patient's house. Wood also was friendly with a domesticated raven that was kept in an ale shop in North Castle Street. Whenever the bird glimpsed the doctor in the distance it would fly to perch on his shoulder.

Although rabbits were hunted and shot as countryside vermin or kept for food, some children were given them as pets. An 1814 painting by the Edinburgh artist Henry Raeburn portrays his step-grandson, Henry Raeburn Inglis, holding a pet white rabbit.

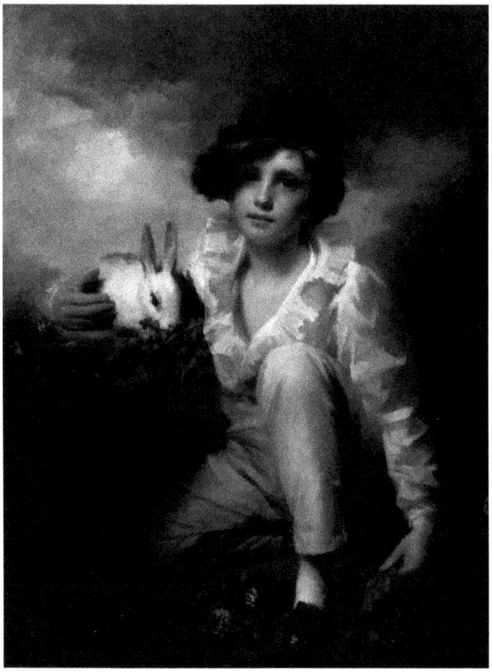

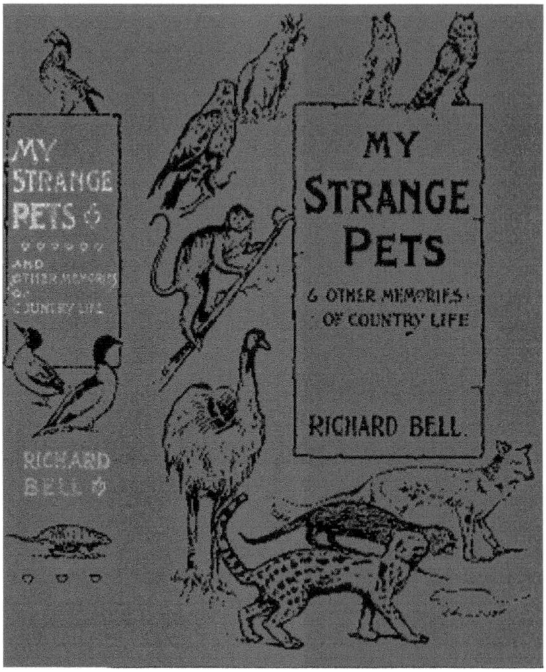

Above left: *Boy and Rabbit* by Sir Henry Raeburn RA, *c.* 1814. (Courtesy of Royal Academy Collection)

Above right: Cover of *My Strange Pets* by Richard Bell.

Inglis was deaf and mute, and despite society's limited understanding of deafness and disabilities at the time, he studied to be a painter.

Richard Bell was born in Edinburgh in 1833 and while studying law at the university attended the natural history classes as he had a deep interest in all animals. In his book *My Strange Pets,* he wrote: 'I have all my life been a lover of pets, and during my younger years these consisted of specimens most easily obtained, and most conveniently and surreptitiously kept in a bedroom or outhouse. As years increased, so increased my ambition and the size of my pets, till these had run from the size of a white mouse to emus.' Although he became a solicitor, his primary interest remained his 'pets' that he mainly kept at his family estate, Castle O'er Hill Fort, in south-west Scotland and he relates his rearing of emus there:

> Emus are rather an expensive stock to lay in. This, however, did not deter me from purchasing a pair as I hoped, if successful, to recoup myself the initial outlay of £20, which was the figure charged me by Mr Charles Jamrach of 180 St George St, East London, the world-famed dealer in wild animals. When they arrived home the children named them Tommy and Jenny ... my breeding experiment succeeded, as I sold 31 young birds, at from £8 to £10 per pair, and received £16 for the original pair when I sold them. And beside this I reaped the profit from the sale of eggs not required for hatching purposes as these are worth 5 shillings each.

In past times many Edinburgh families kept a monkey as a household pet. Monkeys were considered playful, mischievous, adept at mimicry and human-like enough to be regarded by some affectionate owners as no more than naughty children. Indeed, for some, the pet monkey may even have filled the vacant role of child in a childless family. In 1888, Arthur Patterson wrote in *Notes on Pet Monkeys and How to Manage Them*:

> Persons who have a strongly developed propensity for the keeping of pets, have, in most cases, at some time or other, included a monkey in their list of specialties; but with few exceptions, from some mishap or devilry on the part of the little imp, the fancy in that line has come to an abrupt, and, to the rest of the household, a very welcome termination. Such an innate and irrepressible streak of mischief runs through the whole of a monkey's nature that, except under special circumstances, the animal has become branded as an outlaw. Adroitness, agility, restlessness, and mischievous curiosity are their prominent characteristics when in a state of liberty; and in captivity they retain the same, their cunning and comical ways, coupled with inimitable grimace, making them general favourites with the public, especially with the juvenile portion of it.

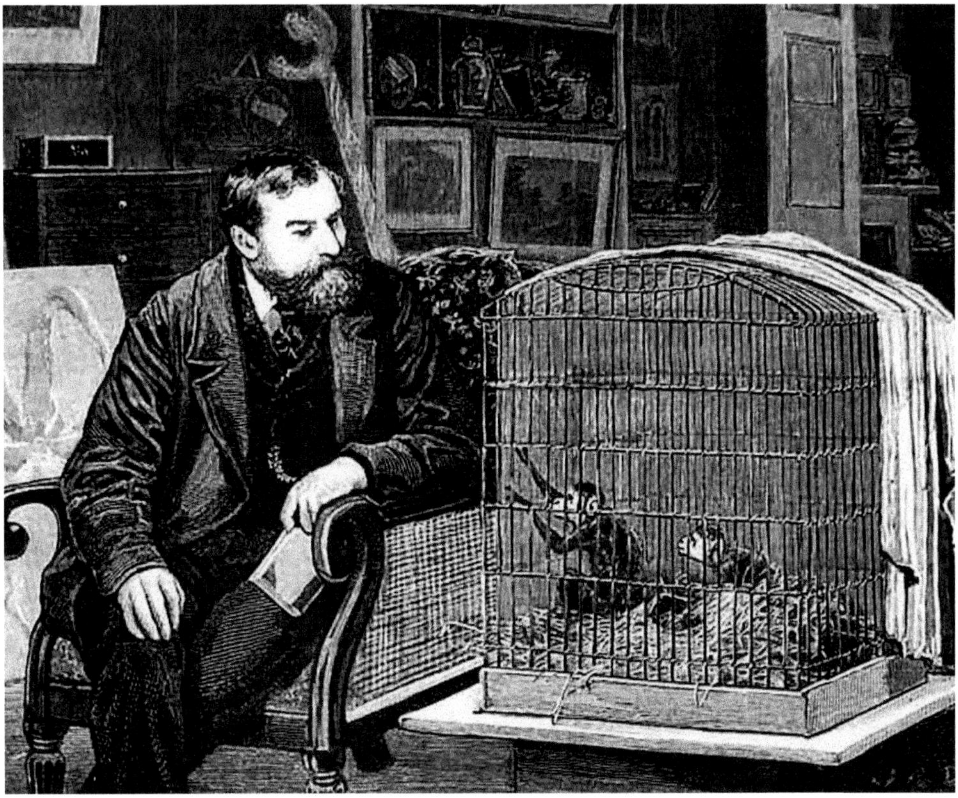

Man with pet monkeys.

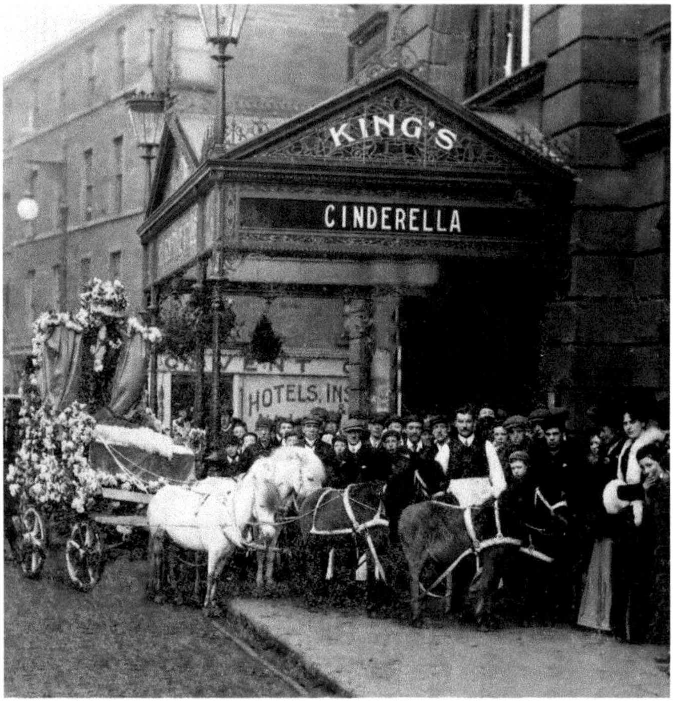

Cinderella coach and Shetland ponies.

Few of those who visited the Bank of Scotland branch in George Street around 1900 and were served by the teller James Wyllie would ever have imagined that the quiet-spoken man could often be seen riding his pet zebra around Currie where he lived. Wyllie trained the animal as part of his informal circus, which included a monkey, a sheep and horses. Every Christmas two of his Shetland ponies regularly appeared in pantomimes in Edinburgh and elsewhere pulling Cinderella's coach.

For a long time Edinburgh's city by-laws prevented the keeping of chickens and hens, yet until the introduction in 1976 of the Dangerous Wild Animals Act there was nothing to prevent anyone from keeping a large wild animal. Around 1975 Meg and Richard Houston, pet shop owners in Edinburgh, came across a lion cub when holidaying in England. They brought the cub back to their shop in Lochrin Place and named it Jason. He lived in a cage at the front of the shop surrounded by more traditional pet shop inhabitants such as tropical fish, budgies, canaries, hamsters and guinea pigs. Mr and Mrs Houston took the young Jason for walks around Tollcross to the delight of passers-by until the police suggested Jason's local walks should end as his increasing size was in danger of alarming unsuspecting members of the public. Jason's popularity drew sightseers to the shop and old ladies would arrive with bags of mince and hand feed Jason through the bars of his cage. However, following the 1976 act, Jason had to leave Tollcross for a zoo in England.

It remains a mystery how a puma came to be resident in Fairley's pub in Leith in the mid-1970s. The puma was kept on a leash next to the bar and on the Go-Go dancing nights would hiss and spit at the dancers and other customers. Unsurprisingly, the area around the puma was avoided by all the pub's clients. The unsuitability of a Leith pub as home

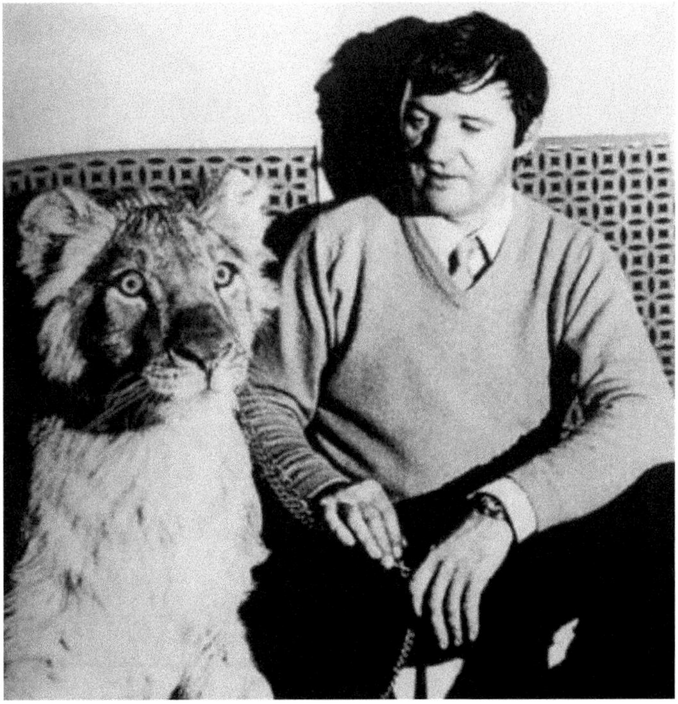

Richard Houston and Jason.

for such an animal was proven one evening when a young woman happened to fall asleep in the toilets and was overlooked when the bar closed. On waking, she went into the bar and was attacked by the puma. Fortunately, her injuries were not life-threatening, but the police removed the puma and the landlord was sacked.

Even a pet parrot can bring a brush with the law. In 2009, the police received a complaint about a parrot called Rio. Local residents objected to the parrot being taken into the garden as it whistled sectarian songs, including 'The Sash', alongside hits from *The King and I*. His owner, a football fan, objected to her parrot being accused of sectarianism and one neighbour said he enjoyed hearing Rio whistle: 'He's amazingly good.' In the end Rio's owner agreed to keep her parrot Rio inside where his full repertoire of tunes would not cause offence. Other bird mimics have also caused irritation. At one menagerie in the 1860s it was noted that 'a petulant magpie kept whistling throughout the exhibition the well-known zoological air, "Pop goes the weasel".'

Times journalist Rachel Compton-Johnson wrote an article in 1997 on the potential pitfalls of keeping exotic pets. She chanced to encounter a distraught boy in her Edinburgh street who told her he had been evicted by his landlord. Uncertain of where he would go, he was worried about his pet, called Dorothy, and Rachel sympathetically offered to house her. 'Dorothy was moved into my flat the next day – a six foot Royal Python in a homemade box. Finding space for her was my first problem but paying electricity bills for the thermal lamp was the second.' On a particularly cold Edinburgh day, she had been out, and returned to find Dorothy freezing cold. Desperate, she wrapped the snake in a pillow case. Although the snake survived, it went off eating and in desperation Rachel

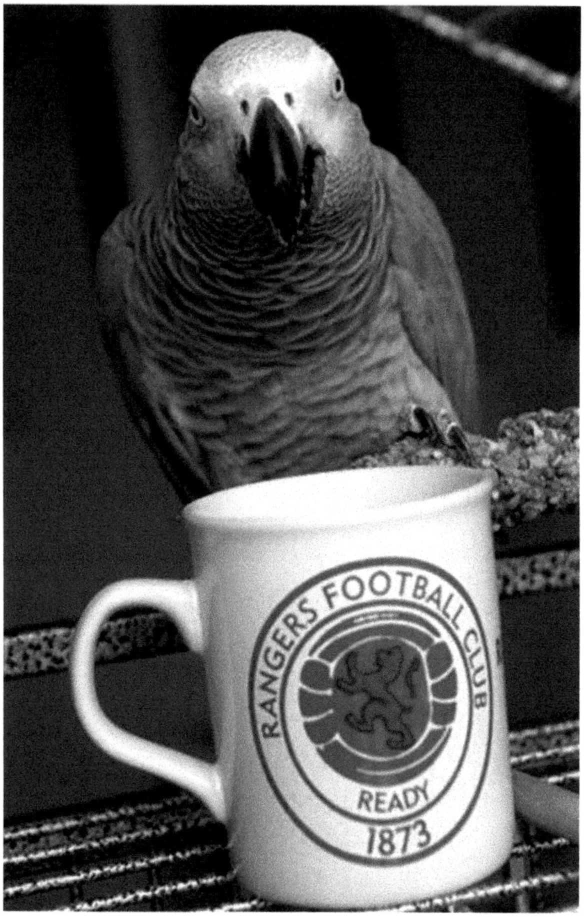

Rio the parrot.

rushed out and bought two gerbils, thinking live food might do the trick. 'Wincingly, I proffered a live gerbil. Five power-packed ounces of desert rat hurtled in terrified attack at my listless reptile. Dorothy ate nothing while a pair of gerbils bred copiously in their cage in the corner of the room.' Eventually, Rachel sensibly rang Edinburgh Zoo, who agreed to take the snake where it lived contentedly, safe from belligerent gerbils.

A more homely pet was suggested in the Edinburgh issue of the student magazine *The Tab*:

> We've all been there – after another glimpse of a cute dog in the Meadows, that familiar feeling bubbles up inside. An urge for a pet. Wouldn't it be nice to have a furry companion to cuddle on cold nights? To sit on your lap while you pull an all-nighter on that essay? Soon, though, reality sets in. Your estate agents are strict, dog food costs too much, and in all honesty, if you can't manage to drag yourself to the gym once a week, how are you meant to commit to taking a small animal out for a walk every day? But whilst a dog is definitely too high-maintenance, what about a more niche pet – a hedgehog, for example?

10. Edinburgh University and Natural History

Edinburgh University has a long and prominent history of researching natural history. In 1697, the university created a permanent display for the natural history specimens that had been collected and donated over the previous decades, so creating one of the first museums in Britain. The collection's reputation spread throughout Europe. Daniel Defoe wrote, 'It is a curious and noble museum.' The diversity and number of items grew significantly in the first half of the nineteenth century, with some 74,000 specimens added through purchases of existing collections or specific items at auctions. As instructions to buy had to be sent by letter, this often led to confusion. In a moment of doubt over one day's purchases at an auction the university's buyer said, 'Today I have perhaps (purchased) too many monkeys.' One visitor to the city in 1790 was delighted to discover the museum:

> In passing along the South Bridge, my attention was caught by a notice projecting from the foot of a stair announcing an exhibition of Birds, Beasts, Fishes, Etc. I expected this to be one of the many itinerant catch penny shows of tigers, lions, monkeys, or dancing dogs but how agreeable it was it to be introduced into a most elegant Museum containing the completest collection of natural curiosities of the animal kind that I have ever beheld.

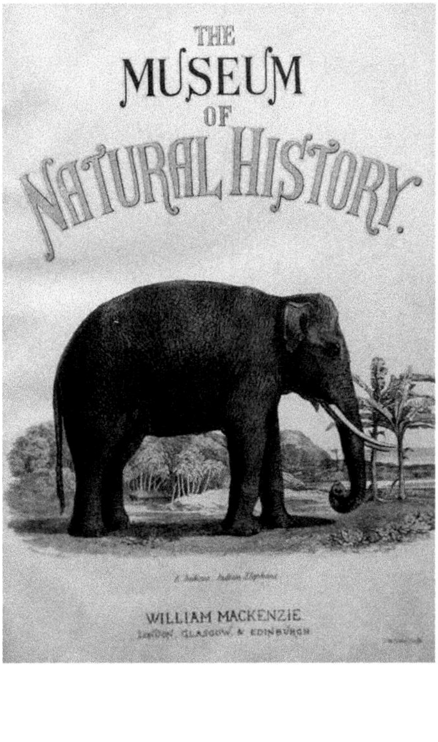

The Museum of Natural History by Sir John Richardson, published in Edinburgh in 1860.

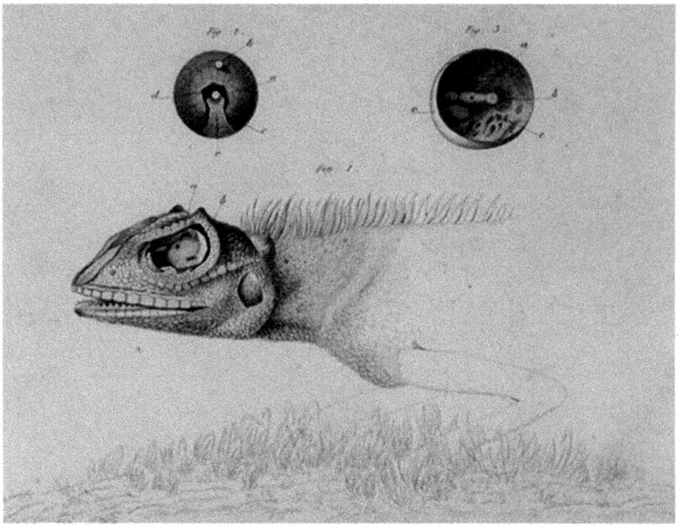

Drawing of duck-billed platypus by Robert Knox.

During the eighteenth and nineteenth centuries a number of Scots, and ex-students of Edinburgh University, undertook scientific travel while others worked across the British Empire. Those with an interest in the natural world remained in touch with Edinburgh University and many sent natural history items for the university's collection. The first European botanical artist to visit Australia was Edinburgh-born Sydney Parkinson, who travelled with Joseph Banks and in 1770 was the first non-Aboriginal to see and sketch a kangaroo. In 1823, Sir Thomas Brisbane, Governor of New South Wales, and an ex-student of Edinburgh University, sent two specimens of the duck-billed platypus to Robert Jameson, the professor of natural history at Edinburgh University. The platypus was of particular interest to natural historians of the time due to its paradoxical mixture of mammalian, avian and reptilian characteristics. When an early specimen arrived in Britain scientists concluded it was probably a fake. Jameson passed one of the mystifying bodies to Robert Knox, a Scottish physician and teacher at the university, for dissection and this rare opportunity brought Knox fame.

William Scoresby, an explorer and scientist, and the inspiration for the character of Lee Scoresby in Philip Pullman's *His Dark Materials,* returned to Britain from a period of exploration in the Arctic in 1812. There he had captured a polar bear cub and during the voyage back Scoresby managed to tame the bear by repeated soft blows to the bear's nose to calm it when it became threatening. On his return Scoresby wintered at the Natural History Department of Edinburgh University to document his discoveries and brought the polar bear with him. As he was keen to observe the bear's behaviours and the progress of its growth, Scoresby had a large hogshead barrel fitted up as a pen in the university's grounds and arranged for the bear to be washed daily with buckets of sea water and fed with a variety of offal. At the end of the winter Scoresby took the bear to London, where it was housed in the menagerie in the Tower of London.

Jameson and Knox, and others teaching at the university such as Robert Edmond Grant, an anatomist and zoologist, were among the most radical thinkers in Britain

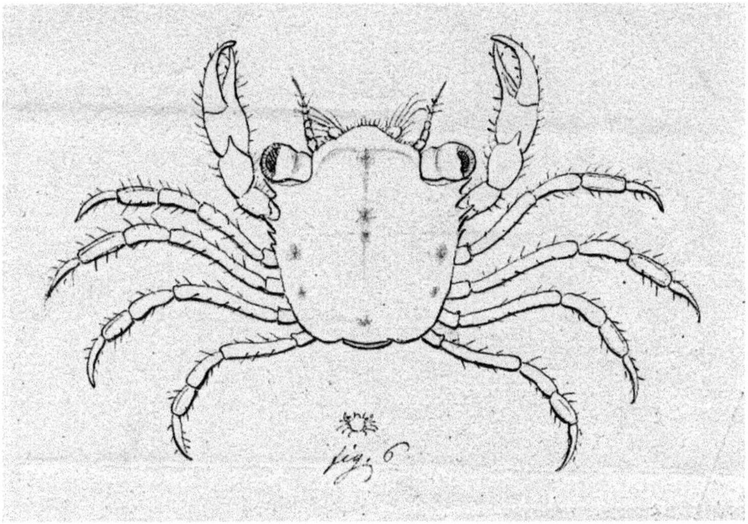

Larva of Cineras vittatus drawn by John Vaughan Thompson, 1836.

at the time, and they passed their innovative ideas on to students. One of the medical students who thus gained a passion for zoology was John Vaughan. He became a military surgeon and a pioneering zoologist. In 1816, he invented the plankton net 'which brought up such a profusion of other marine animals altogether invisible while in the sea, as to induce a continued use of it on every favourable opportunity'. Thompson published his research in a series of six memoirs from 1828 to 1834 and although many of his discoveries were ground-breaking, including being the first to show that barnacles are crustaceans rather than molluscs, most of his findings were ignored; museum professionals considered him an amateur and thus he did not receive credit during his lifetime.

A number of significant natural history societies were instituted in the city. The Plinian Natural History Society provided a forum where ideas such as phrenology and the transmutation of species were eagerly discussed. When Charles Darwin was studying medicine at Edinburgh University from 1826 to 1827, he was a member and those he met there influenced his thinking. In 1808, Jameson founded the Wernerian Society that discussed and published papers on natural history, and included many notable scientists of the time.

At a meeting of the Wernerian society in 1809, Charles Stewart provided a list of the insects found by him in the neighbourhood of Edinburgh. The list contained about 400 species, only a few of which he judged rare. Stewart explained that his insect collecting had been carried out over two years 'and without very favourable opportunities. My list is produced merely as an incitement to younger and jealous etymologists'. It was not only etymologists that travelled far and wide to study and pin down the diversity of the animal world, but the National Museum Scotland's entomology collection of nearly 2 million specimens shows they were particularly industrious The sheer scale of this trawl of the world's insects brings to mind the 'shepherd boy' in a poem by

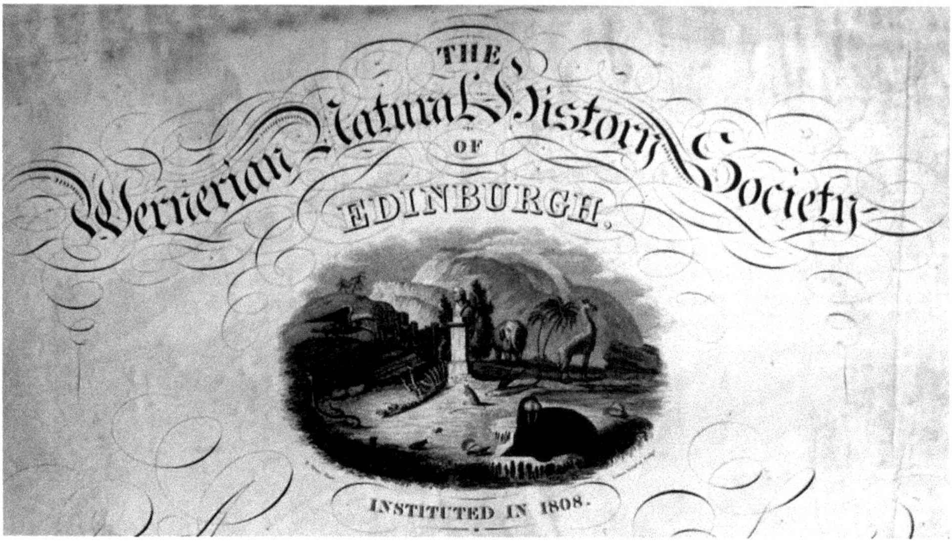

Wernerian Natural History Society of Edinburgh membership certificate, 1831.

Robert Ferguson, the eighteenth-century Edinburgh poet whose work inspired Robert Burns:

At noontide, as Colin and Sylvia lay
Within a cool jessamine bower,
A butterfly, waked by the heat of the day.
Was sipping the juice of each flower.
Near the shade of this covert, a young shepherd boy
The gaudy brisk flutterer spies.
Who held it as pastime to seek and destroy
Each beautiful insect that flies.

This widespread collecting was carried out to help understand the animal world better, and by displaying the finds to inspire the wider public to appreciate the diversity of the animal kingdom. The growth of Edinburgh University's animal and bird collections required taxidermists and a number of reputed 'bird stuffers', as they were then described, worked in the city. One was John Edmonstone, a freed black slave who initially came to Scotland as a servant to Charles Edmonstone whose plantation he had worked on. He learnt taxidermy in Guyana from Charles Waterton, an eccentric landowner and naturalist, and in 1823 set up in business. He also gave lessons in taxidermy to medical students from the university, one of whom was the young Charles Darwin, who wrote: 'I am going to learn to stuff birds, from a blackamoor. It has the recommendation of cheapness, if it has nothing else, as he only charges one guinea, for an hour every day for two months.'

In 1866, the collections from the University Natural History Museum were transferred to the new Museum of Science and Art and as many of the stuffed animals, especially mammals, 'stood greatly in need of renewal', taxidermists were kept busy. Those, and later, collections are now housed in the National Museums Scotland.

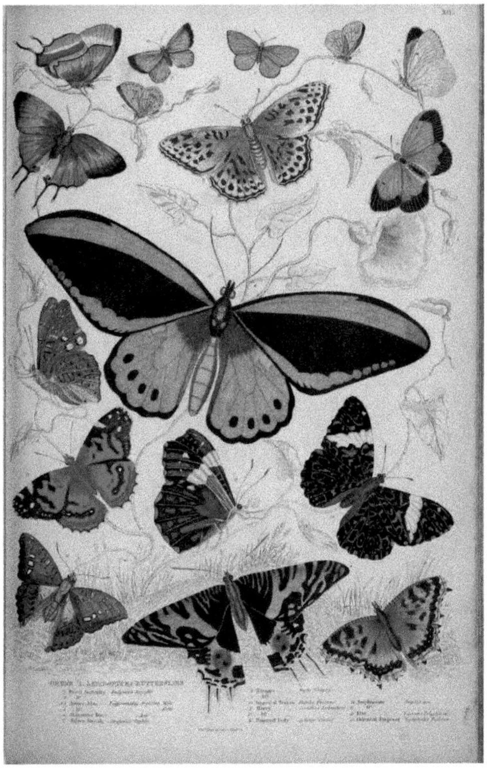

Right: Illustration of butterflies from the *Edinburgh Journal of Natural History*.

Below: Taxidermy workroom, National Museum of Natural History, 1911. (Courtesy of Smithsonian Institution Archives)

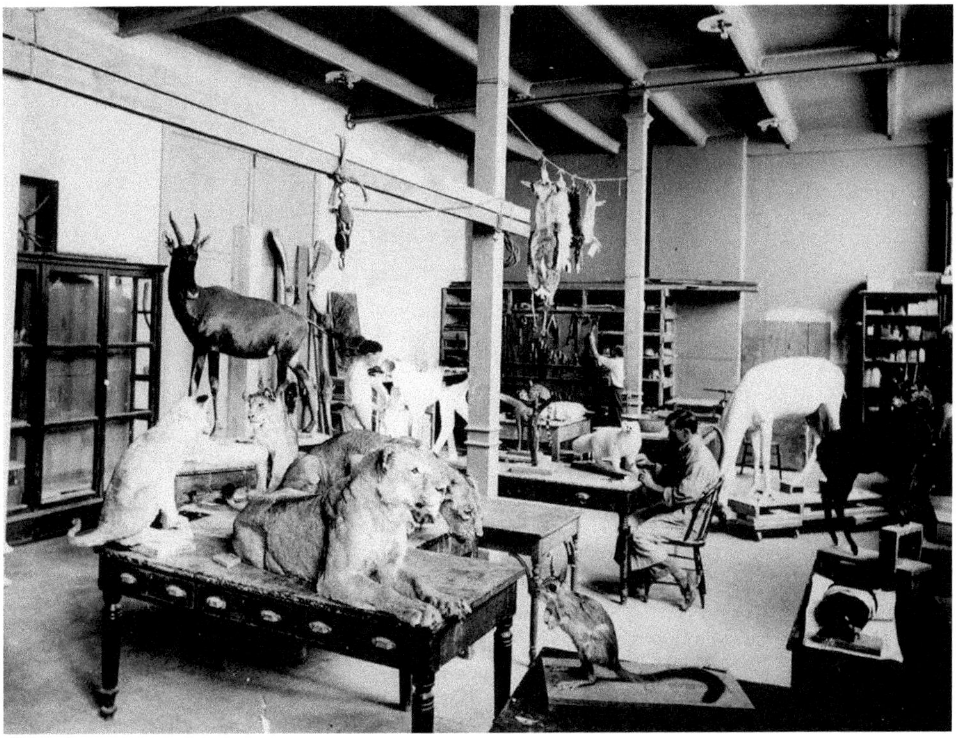

The fashion for taxidermy could be bad news for birds. In 1845, a hoopee bird made a rare appearance in Fife, probably having been blown off course while migrating to Africa, and was shot by a landowner who delivered 'this stray wanderer from the sedgy banks of the Nile into the hands of Mr Carfrae, bird-stuffer in Edinburgh'.

In 1831, a dead blue whale was spotted by a ship off Bass Rock and towed to the beach at North Berwick. Robert Knox wished to preserve the skeleton so over a week a team of labourers cut away the blubber and removed it by horse and cart. The skeleton measured 78 feet in length and weighed 2 tons. After three years preparation the skeleton was exhibited in the Royal Institution. In 1840, it was lent to the new zoo in Claremont Street and exhibited in a building paid for by the city. Almost twenty years later the city council were alarmed to read an advert offering the whale skeleton for sale. The city swiftly repossessed the whale from the zoo and in 1866 presented it to the newly opened Edinburgh Museum of Science and Art in Chambers Street, where it was a cherished exhibit until its removal in 2011 as part of the museum's refurbishment.

The Edinburgh Journal of Natural History, and of the Physical Sciences was published from 1835 to 1840 and the introduction to the first edition stated:

> The taste for Natural History is now universally diffused throughout the empire ... The enormous price at which illustrations of a higher order are usually sold, has alone prevented them from becoming extensively popular. Hitherto, coloured engravings, executed with beauty and correctness, have been accessible to the wealthier classes alone. It is proposed, in this work, to place elegant engravings of the choicest productions of Nature, within the reach of all classes of the community; and thus, in small towns and in the country, where museums are unknown, and libraries very scarce: the lover of Nature will be enabled to extend his knowledge of the works of the Creator beyond the limited sphere of his own observations.

In 1895, James Cossar Ewart, Edinburgh University's Regius Professor of Natural History, established a 'Natural History Station' in Penicuik, 10 miles south of the city. There he carried out cross-breeding experiments, including cross-breeding zebras and horses to create zebroids, and his work contributed to the various investigations into heredity taking place around Britain at the time. He wrote about one of his zebras, called Matopo:

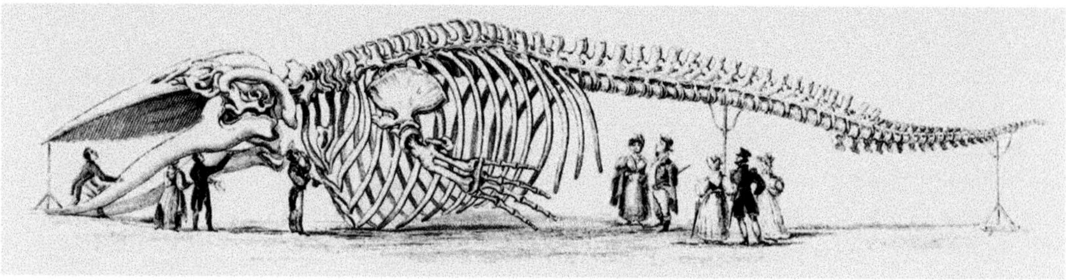

The Edinburgh Whale in the Royal Institution on the Mound.

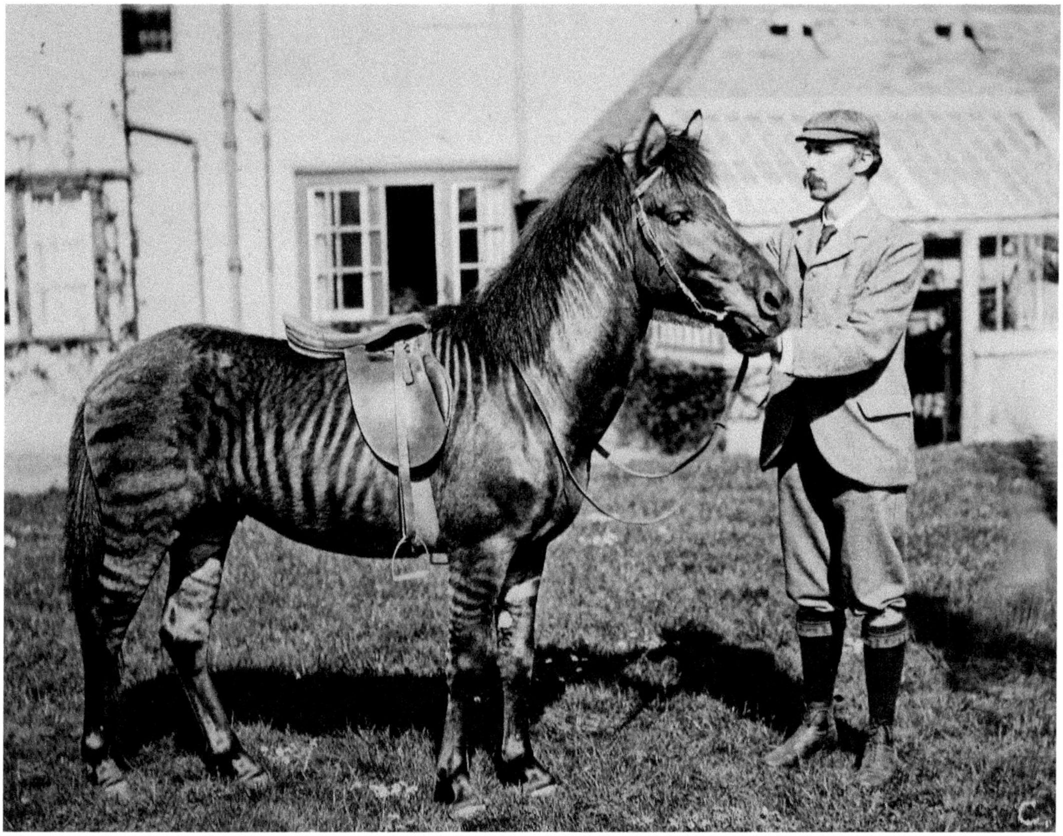

James Cossar Ewart with a zebroid *c.* 1910.

> A zebra is in all respects more intense than a horse, he is more on the alert, more timid and suspicious, and yet more imbued with curiosity. When he once decides to take action he moves more rapidly than a horse, is more regardless of consequences, and usually suffers less from an injury than from the shock to his nervous system. One evening, when Matopo had refused for hours to retire into his box, I threw a rug over him. He bounded across the court, first nearly upsetting a mare, and then nearly breaking his neck against the fence, and then rushed around his box until the dreaded object was got rid of. Had it been a lion the panic could hardly have been greater, but he soon learned that a rug, however suggestive, was perfectly harmless.

In 1919, Edinburgh University established a Chair of Zoology and a year later the first lectureship in genetics. As a result, in 1920 the government chose Edinburgh as the location for the first national centre for animal breeding research with the aim of applying the emerging science of genetics to the improvement of livestock and agricultural production. Over the next two decades the small experimental 'station' was transformed into the university's Institute of Animal Genetics and it attracted leading geneticists. The work of the institute was diverse, from classical genetics using drosophila fruit flies to large-scale livestock experiments. Dr Fraser Darling, who worked at the institute in the 1920s and 1930s, recounted his fondness for the Shetland sheep that formed part of the research farm: 'They have wisdom which other sheep have lost; they have primitive grace and their soft chestnut-coloured "moorit" wool gives them a most satisfying appearance.'

Appropriately, it was a sheep that brought international fame to Edinburgh's genetics work. The Roslin Institute, which had emerged out of the Institute of Animal Genetics, began experimenting on animal cloning and on 5 July 1996 a lamb was born that was the first-ever animal to be cloned from an adult cell. The ground-breaking work was carried out by Keith Campbell, Ian Wilmut and colleagues, and Wilmut explained why the sheep had been named Dolly: 'She is derived from a mammary gland cell and we couldn't think of a more impressive pair of glands than Dolly Parton's (the famous country and western singer). Dolly later was bred with a Welsh mountain ram, producing six lambs during her six-year life. She died in February 2003, but her preserved body can be seen at the National Museum Scotland.

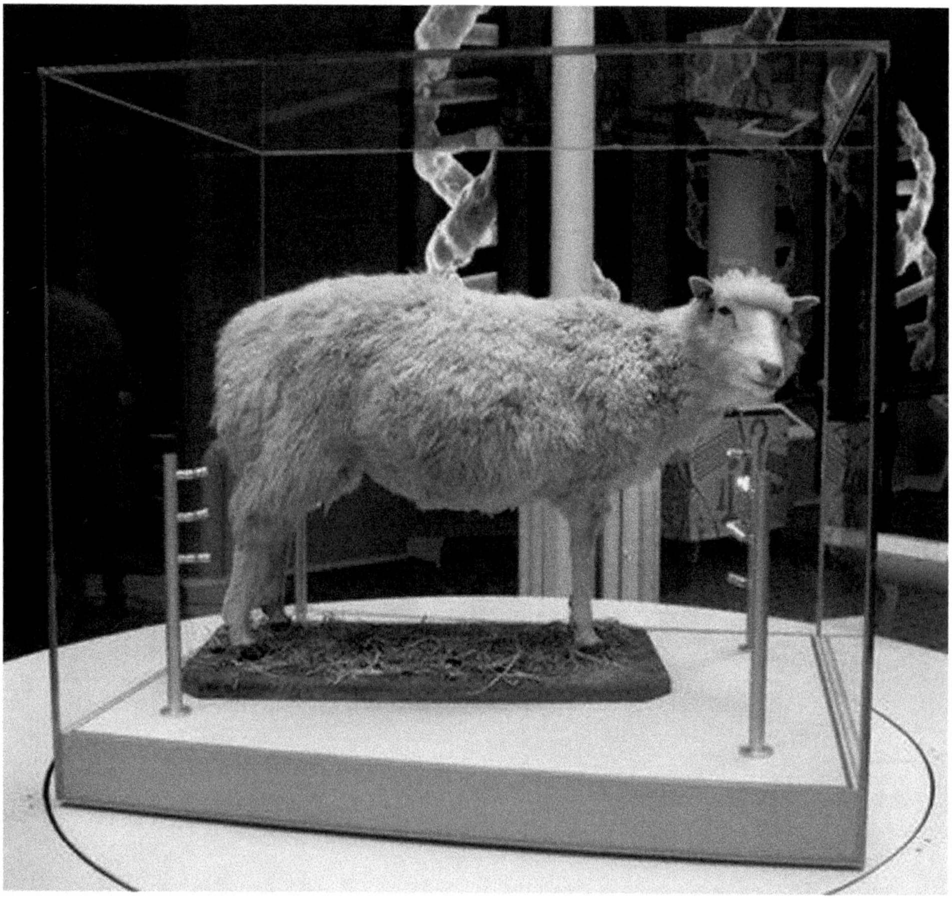

Dolly the sheep.

11. Animal Portraits

Edinburgh's streets and buildings are home to a variety of animal sculptures, and, uniquely, five are of named dogs. That the city contains fewer statues to named women is, understandably, considered unjust. The most famous of the dog statues, and generally considered the most iconic canine statue in the world, is Greyfriars Bobby, outside Greyfriars Kirk. At the bottom of the Scott Monument, Maida sits at the feet of Sir Walter Scott; in George Street, Toby keeps James Clerk Maxwell company; outside Colinton Church, Coolin tries to climb on to the knee of Robert Louis Stevenson; and inside the Kings Stables Road entrance to Princes Street Gardens lies a statue of Bum, a dog that lived in San Diego in the 1880s and 1890s. This statue was presented to Edinburgh by San Diego in 2008 as, like Edinburgh's Greyfriars Bobby, Bum also was a favourite stray and he too had his dog licence paid for by the city. Two nameless dogs can be seen on the moving Scottish American War Memorial in Princes Street Gardens West created by

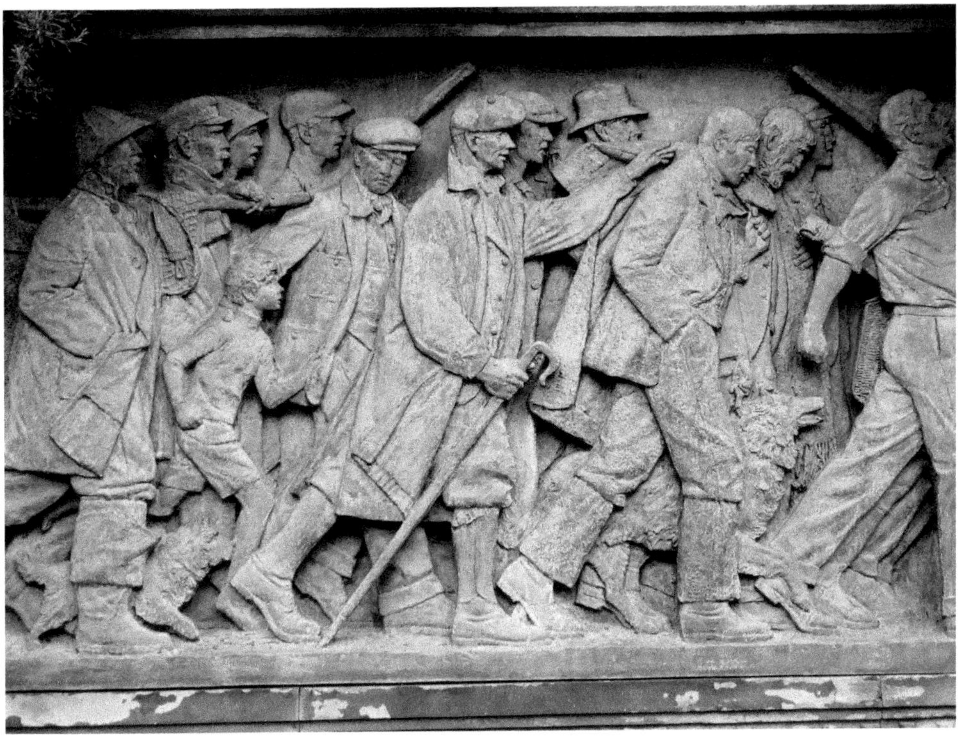

Terrier and collie dogs – detail from *American War Memorial* by Robert Tait Mackenzie, Princes Street Gardens East.

Robert Tait Mackenzie, a Scots Canadian. The bas relief depicts Scottish working men marching off to the war and among their feet are a terrier and a collie, both apparently determined to accompany their masters into battle. Given the large numbers of soldiers who never returned from war, these possibly symbolise all the dogs that pined in vain for their masters' return.

There are numerous fine equestrian statues, although only one portrays a named horse. This is the bronze statue of the Duke of Wellington that was made by John Steell and is sited outside Register House at the east end of Princes Street. The duke sits astride Copenhagen, his favourite steed. The earliest, and reputedly the oldest, lead equestrian statue in the United Kingdom is a life-sized statue of Charles II that sits in Parliament Square, behind St Giles Cathedral. It was erected in 1685, the year of the king's death, and depicts him in Roman military garb astride a horse. The fashion for depicting celebrated men in Roman clothing extended to Thomas Campbell's 1824 equestrian statue of Lord Hopeton outside Dundas House in St Andrew Square. Hopeton is shown on horseback as he served in the dragoons. Another striking equestrian sculpture is the 1906 memorial to the soldiers of the Royal Scots Greys by William Birnie Rhind that stands above West Princes Street Gardens

Another Steell equestrian statue in the courtyard of the City Chambers portrays the moment that Alexander the Great pacified the apparently untameable horse, Bucephalus, by forcing the horse towards the sun, having realised it was the horse's own shadow that caused it distress. Steell created a maquette in 1832 but was not paid. The infuriated artist is reputed to have replaced the original horse's ears with those modelled from a pig and some believe that when Steell's sculpture was eventually cast fifty years later it still sported its 'pig's ears', though whether the city council were sold a pig in a poke is for

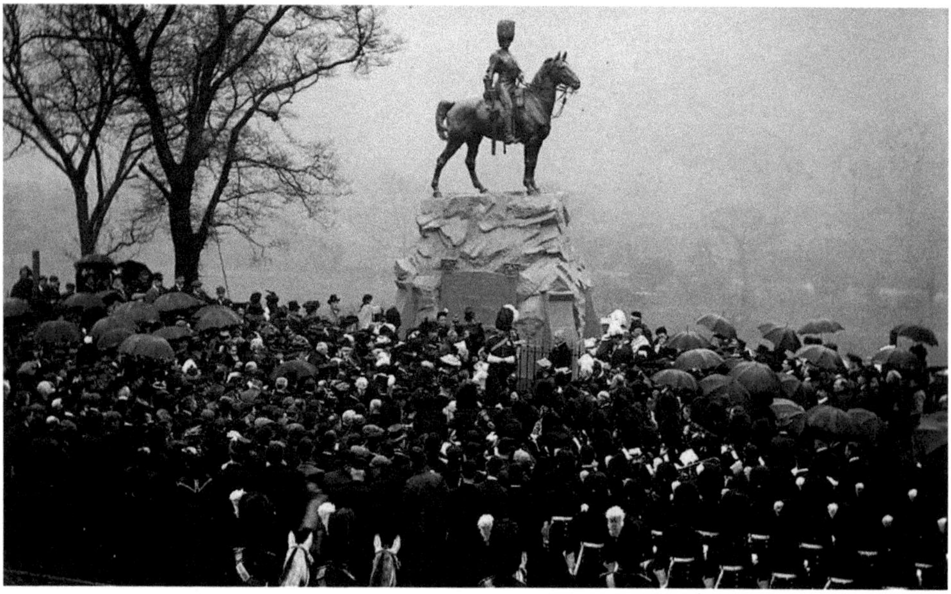

Unveiling the Scots Grey Memorial statue in 1906.

the viewer to decide. A 1993 portrayal of the Bucephalus myth by Eoghan Bridge can be found in Rutland Court walkway in Fountainbridge.

Many lions grace Edinburgh's streets. Jill Watson's imposing sculpture above the entrance to the Queen's Gallery at Holyrood Palace of a red lion with blue tongue and claws was created in 2002 and draws its inspiration from a small red lion that sits at the feet of Mary, Queen of Scots on her tomb in Westminster Abbey. The oldest depiction of a lion in the city dates from the Roman occupation, long before Scotland evolved into a nation. It was discovered in 1997 lying in the bed of the River Almond at Cramond. The imposing Roman monument depicts a lioness sinking her teeth into the skull of a naked captive, probably a local Caledonian, and can be viewed in the Museum of Scotland. The most recent lion sculpture is Ronald Rae's impressive *Lion of Scotland*, which reclines in St Andrew Square. The most unusual image of a lion is on David Livingstone's statue in Princes Street Gardens East. This includes a slain lion and denotes the time when Livingstone shot but did not kill the animal. The wounded animal savaged Livingstone before it was killed by a spear and as a result he lost the use of his left arm. The statue was made in 1875 by Amelia Robertson Hill and is one of the few in Edinburgh sculpted by a woman.

The coat of arms of the Canongate features a white stag's head and a golden cross, and the one on the top of Canongate Church has real antlers that came from a stag shot at Balmoral by King George VI in 1949. Six rampant stags form part of the 1888 memorial to the Duke of Buccleuch that sits next to St Giles Cathedral. This memorial also includes a number of bas-reliefs of horses.

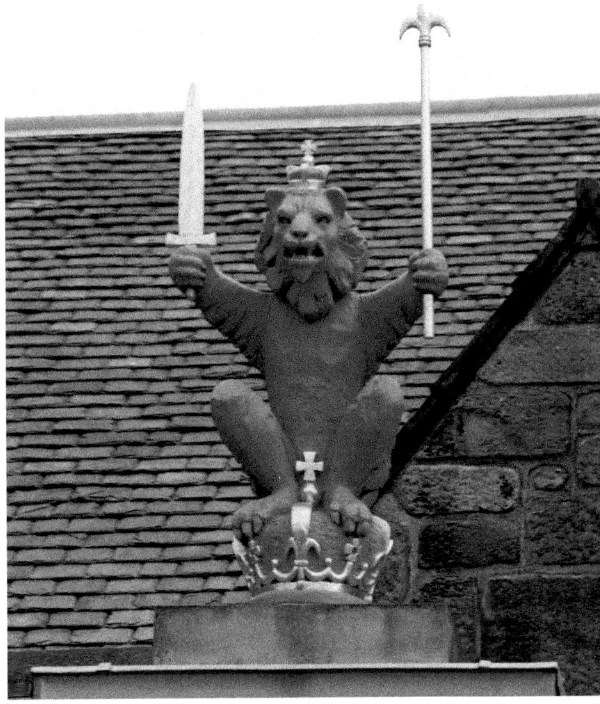

Scottish lion by Jill Watson, Queen's Gallery, Palace of Holyroodhouse.

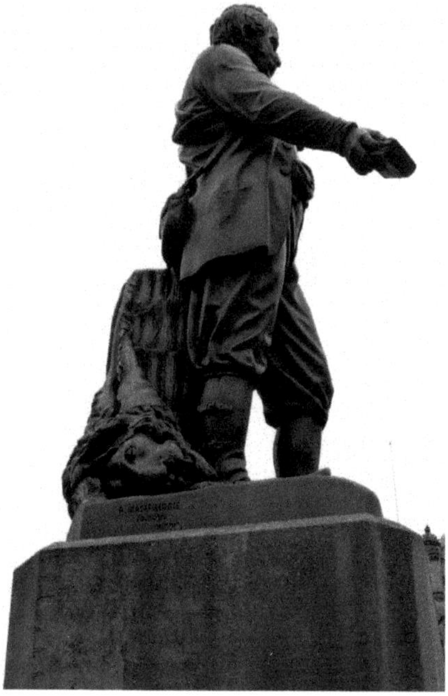

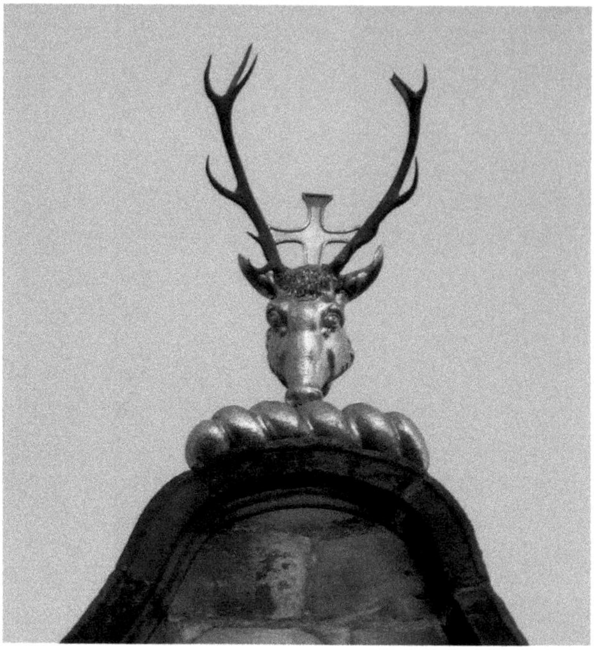

Above left: Dead lion and Stanley Livingstone by Amelia Robertson Hill, Princes Street Gardens West.

Above right: Canongate emblem on top of Canongate Kirk.

Although cats have long been kept as pets and to ward off the city's many mice and rats, not one is represented among the city's many animal sculptures. It is often thought one sits high up on the roof of Ramsay Garden on Castlehill and while the sculpture appears very cat-like, it is actually a Devil in disguise. When Patrick Geddes designed the Ramsay Garden buildings in the 1890s he added three terracotta sculptures to the roofs: an angel, a sphinx and 'Auld Nick'. However, the lofty position of the sculptures resulted in the angel and sphinx being blown away and although the Devil clung on, it lost its original wings, transforming it into a quasi-cat.

In Cockburn Street, high up on Nos 67 to 71, is an attractive bas relief depicting two monkeys, a chameleon, a parrot and another ferocious cat-like beast grasping the tail of a snake. Another snake can be found on the Witches' Well that is at the top of the Royal Mile. The Witches' Well commemorate the Scots women who, without trial, were burned as witches between the fifteenth and eighteenth centuries. The image of a snake entwined with two witches' heads was created by John Duncan in 1894.

In the castle esplanade is a monument commemorating the soldiers of the 78th Ross-shire Highland Regiment who died in India during the suppression of the Indian Rebellion. It shows an elephant and a stag, the former being added to the regiment's armorial decoration in honour of its part in the Battle of Assaye in 1803. A recent baby elephant sculpture in Princes Street Gardens West marks quite a different loss. It is a memorial to the children whose ashes were buried or disposed of secretly at Mortonhall

Crematorium over decades, despite parents being told there were no remains of their children. Designed by Andy Scott in association with the grieving parents, it is named Lulla-Bye.

Sculpted owls and squirrels can be found on the exterior of the Scottish Portrait Gallery on Queen Street, but the building with the greatest number of carved creatures is the delightful Venetian building that is hidden away in nearby West Register Street Lane. Over twenty birds and other animals sit amid carved foliage on the three façades of this ornate Gothic-style building that was designed by W. Hamilton Beattie in 1864. Its grand name and flamboyant exterior belies its original use as a paper warehouse for Cowans, a papermaking company.

Cockerels lord it over many of the city's churches and it is thought that the representation of a cockerel on church weathervanes stems from the sixth century when Pope Gregory I declared that the cock was the animal most worthy of symbolising Christianity, as it represented Jesus' prophecy that the cock would not crow in the morning until Peter denounced Him three times. In a city as windy as Edinburgh weathervanes take a buffeting and in 1667 the gilded one on St Giles' Cathedral's had to be replaced. Alexander Anderson, a coppersmith, was commissioned to create the replacement and clearly did

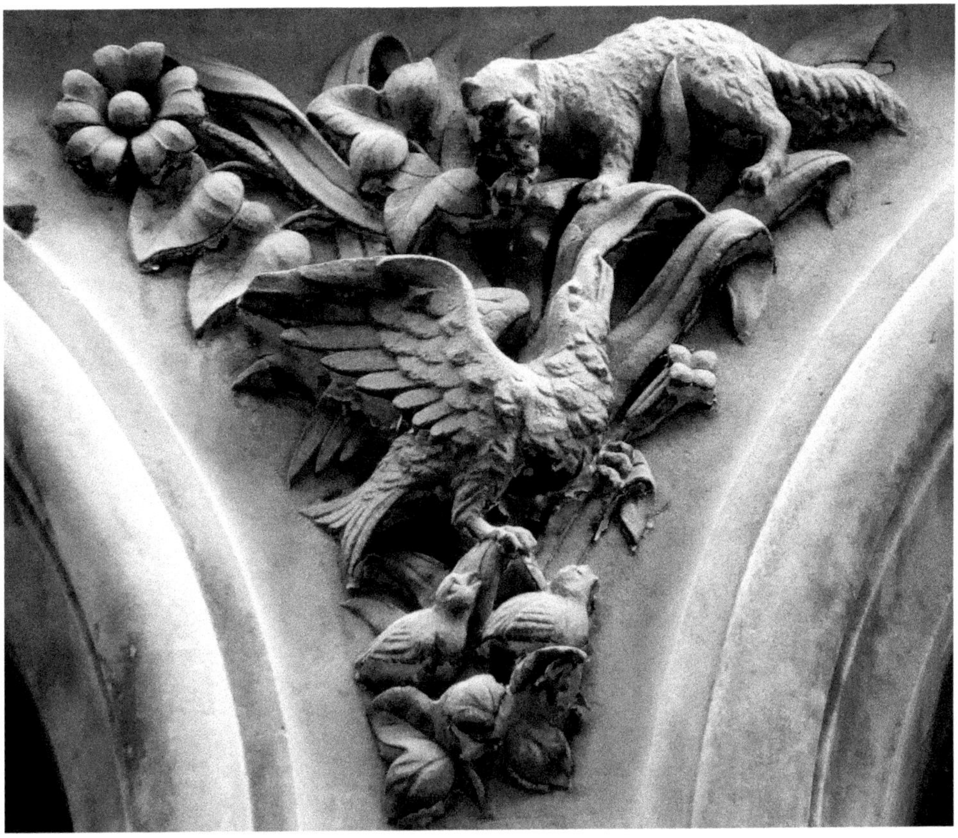

Sculpture on the façade of the Venetian building by W. Hamilton Beattie, West Register Street.

an excellent job, for his withstood the elements until 1979, when a strong gale almost brought the cockerel and part of the steeple crashing down. Fortunately, Anderson's weathercock survived, and after repair and re-gilding was returned to its accustomed perch. A delightful sculpture of a cockerel astride a trumpet can be found in Bakehouse Close, opposite Canongate Kirk. Sir Archibald Acheson, a government minister for Charles I, had the mansion erected in 1633 and adorned with his family crest – a cockerel and a trumpet. However, Acheson was unable to enjoy his new town house for long, as he died the year after it was finished.

The sculpture of the two giraffes – a mother and her calf – that stands outside the Omni Centre in Leith Walk was created by Helen Denerley in 2005 from scrap metal, including parts from cars and motorbikes. The artist named her sculpture *Dreaming Spires*, a term taken from a nineteenth-century poem by Matthew Arnold in reference to Oxford's skyline as she thought it equally appropriate to Edinburgh's dreaming spires, although she also nicknamed the two giraffes Martha and Gilbert.

One of the most recent animal sculptures, and already a tourist favourite, is a memorial to the Polish bear, Wojtek, in Princes Street Gardens West, created by Alan Beattie Herriot in 2015. Wojtek was bought by Polish soldiers in 1942 and became the 22nd Artillery Supply Company's mascot, and much indulged in his fondness for beer and eating cigarettes. Due to regulations forbidding animals being taken to the front line,

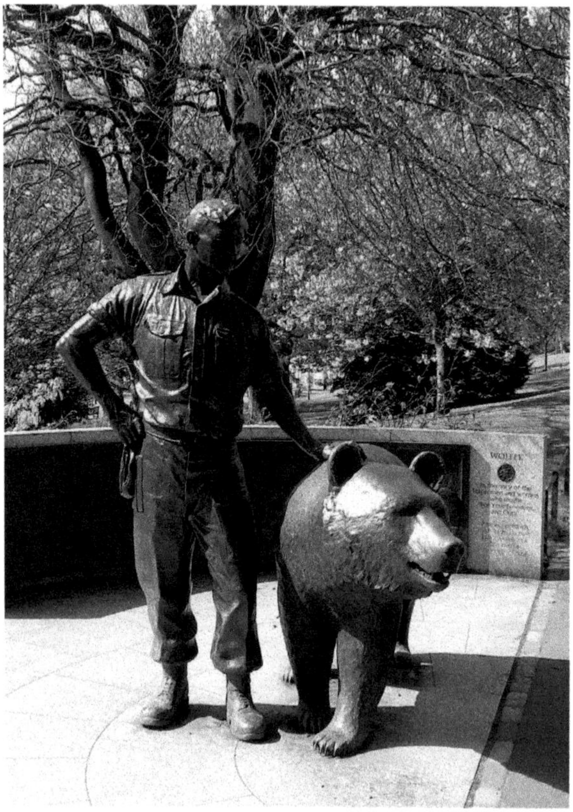

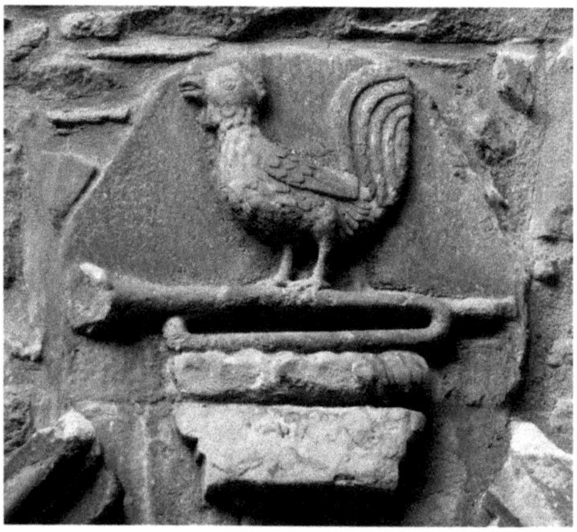

Above: Acheson family crest plaque dated 1633 in Bakehouse Close.

Left: Memorial to Wojtek the Polish bear, by Alan Beattie Herriot in Princes Street Gardens East.

the platoon issued Wojtek with a rank and serial number, and he was with them during the Battle of Monte Cassino. Wojtek observed soldiers moving crates and began to help by carrying ammunition up to the guns – never dropping a single crate. After the war the Polish Platoon and Wojtek were temporarily housed in Scotland and when the soldiers returned home in 1947 Wojtek was given to Edinburgh Zoo. He was a frequent guest on BBC Television's children's programme *Blue Peter.*

An unusual sculpture of a rhinoceros head emerging from the wall of the University's Informatics Forum, off Bristo Square was made by William Darrell and refers to another rhino head that was affixed to Jim Haynes' bookshop, Paperback, which was sited in George Square in the 1950s and 1960s. Haynes was a key figure in Edinburgh's alternative cultural scene, including establishing the Traverse Theatre. The bookshop's famous rhinoceros head was procured in 1960 when Haynes happened to be walking down Princes Street. Outside the private gentlemen-only New Club he encountered two workmen carrying out the mounted rhino and, on being told it was to be thrown away, took it and affixed it to the front of his bookshop.

The smallest animal represented in a public sculpture is a bee. A number are included in the sculpture honouring Sir Patrick Geddes created in 2012 by Kenny Hunter that can be found in Sandeman House Garden, off the High Street. Geddes was a Scottish visionary whose innovative approaches to town planning in Edinburgh's rundown Old Town created improved living conditions, while retaining the existing character of historic buildings. Geddes lectured on Zoology at Edinburgh University and wrote about the vital role of bees in ecology. He was a strong advocate of nature conservation and his ideas were a forerunner of the concept 'think globally, act locally'.

Robert Burns' famous lines, 'The best-laid schemes o' mice an' men gang aft agley', is reflected in the one sculpture of a mouse in the city, for the little mouse is clutched in the talons of a hawk on the gilded sign that hangs outside Gladstone's Land in the Lawnmarket.

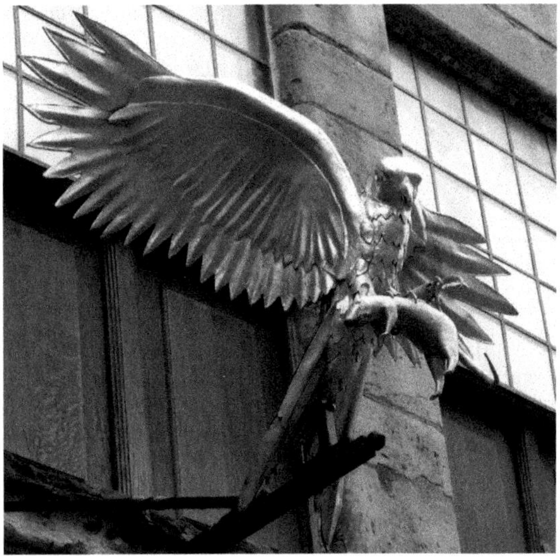

Hawk and mouse sign, Gladstones Land, Lawnmarket.

Two cows and sheep are included in the sculptural frieze that is on the upper storey of the building on the west side of Parliament Square. The building was originally the offices of Midlothian County and the frieze by the sculptor William Birnie Rhind represents the industries of Midlothian at the time: agriculture, fishing and mining.

In 1919, Edinburgh University instituted a Chair of Zoology and ten years later the Department of Zoology (now Ashworth Laboratories) opened in a new building in West Mains Road. On the exterior are a series of oval plaques sculpted by Phyllis Bone, the first female Royal Scottish Academician. These show animals from each of the principal zoogeographical regions and included are a reindeer, aardvark, a dung beetle and an octopus. Phyllis Bone also sculpted the animals that are portrayed under the banner, 'Remember also the Humble Beasts', in the Scottish National War Memorial in Edinburgh Castle. The animals commemorated include an elephant, a horse, a rescue dog, carrier pigeons and 'the tunnellers' friends'; canaries and mice that were used to give warning of methane or carbon dioxide.

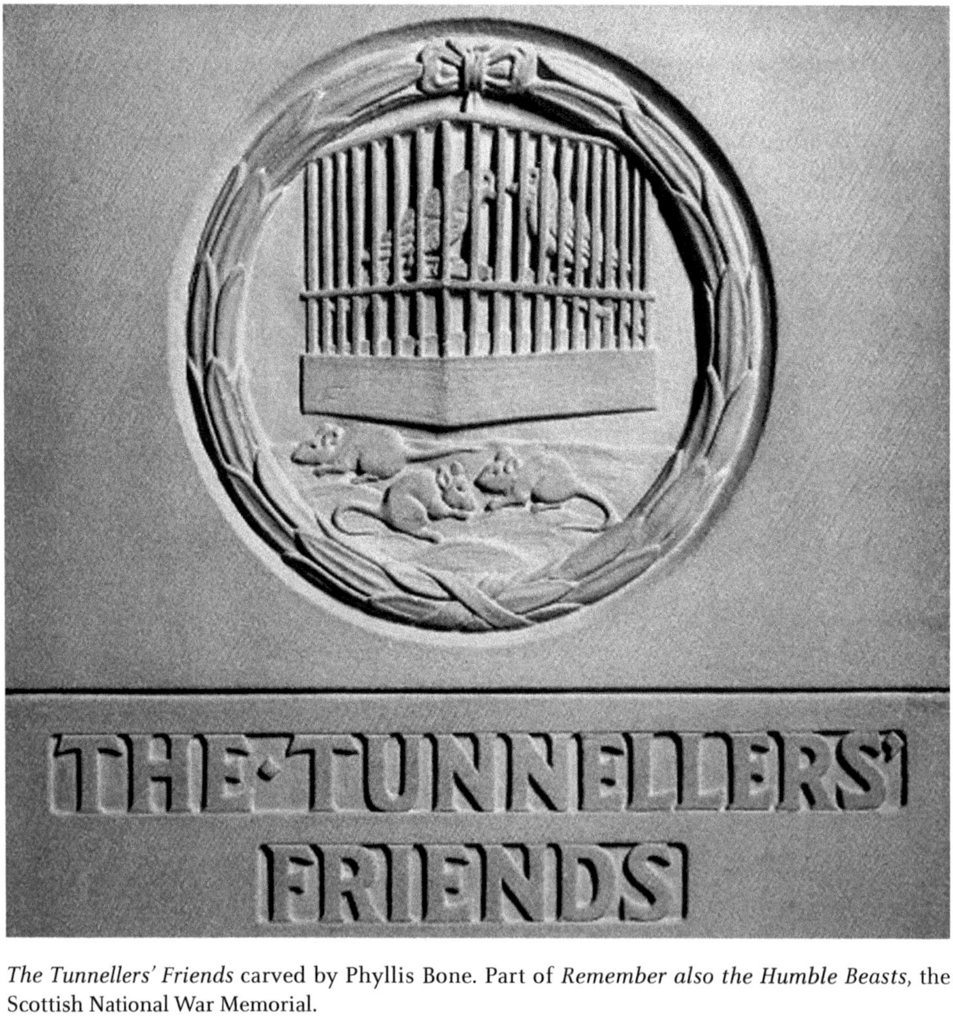

The Tunnellers' Friends carved by Phyllis Bone. Part of *Remember also the Humble Beasts*, the Scottish National War Memorial.